It's About Time!

CAROLYN CASTLEBERRY

It's About Time!

10 Smart Strategies to Avoid Time Traps

and Invest Yourself Where It Matters

HOWARD BOOKS
A DIVISION OF SIMON & SCHUSTER
NEW YORK LONDON TORONTO SYDNEY

Our purpose at Howard Books is to:
- *Increase faith* in the hearts of growing Christians
- *Inspire holiness* in the lives of believers
- *Instill hope* in the hearts of struggling people everywhere

Because He's coming again!

Published by Howard Books, a division of Simon & Schuster, Inc.,
1230 Avenue of the Americas, New York, NY 10020
www.howardpublishing.com

It's About Time! © 2009 by Carolyn Castleberry

Published in association with Ambassador Literary Agency, Nashville, Tennessee

Library of Congress Cataloging-in-Publication Data
It's about time : 10 smart strategies to avoid time traps and invest yourself where it matters / Carolyn Castleberry.
   p. cm.
Includes bibliographical references.
1. Time management—Religious aspects—Christianity. I. Title.
BV4598.5.C37 2009
640'.43—dc22

                                        2008037381

ISBN-13: 978-1-4165-6845-2

10   9   8   7   6   5   4   3   2   1

HOWARD and colophon are registered trademarks of Simon & Schuster, Inc.

Manufactured in the United States of America
For information regarding special discounts for bulk purchases,
please contact: Simon & Schuster Special Sales at 1-800-456-6798
or business@simonandschuster.com.

Edited by Lisa Bergren and Cindy Lambert

Interior design by Jaime Putorti
Photography/illustrations by Michael Wade Studios, Va. Beach

Extract on page 105 is from Annie's Mailbox® by Kathy Mitchell and Marcy Sugar, distributed by Creators Syndicate. Used by permission.

Scripture quotations marked NASB are from the *New American Standard Bible*®. Copyright © 1960, 1962, 1963, 1968, 1971, 1972, 1973, 1975, 1977, 1995 by The Lockman Foundation. Used by permission. Scripture quotations marked NIV are from the *Holy Bible, New International Version*®. Copyright © 1973, 1978, 1984 by International Bible Society. Used by permission of Zondervan. All rights reserved. Scripture quotations marked NLT are from the *Holy Bible, New Living Translation,* copyright © 1996, 2004. Used by permission of Tyndale House Publishers, Inc., Wheaton, Illinois 60189. All rights reserved. Scripture quotations marked MSG are from *The Message.* Copyright © 1993, 1994, 1995, 1996, 2000, 2001, 2002. Used by permission of NavPress Publishing Group. All rights reserved. Scripture quotations marked CEV are taken from the *Contemporary English Version,* copyright © 1995 by the American Bible Society. Scripture quotations marked NLV are taken from the *New Life Version,* copyright © 1969 by Christian Literature International. Scriptures marked NIRV are taken from the *Holy Bible, New International Reader's Version*®. Copyright © 1996, 1998 International Bible Society. All rights reserved throughout the world. Used by permission of International Bible Society. Scripture quotations marked *The Book* are taken from *The Book* version of the *New Living Translation,* copyright © 1996, 2004. Used by permission of Tyndale House Publishers, Inc., Wheaton, Illinois 60189. All rights reserved.

To my parents, Len and Ruth Anderson,
who have given me the greatest gift they have—their time

CONTENTS

PART THREE

INVESTING TIME AND TALENTS

It's About Time!

I can see you there now. In the bookstore, at a friend's house, open-ing this book and thinking *I don't have time for this*. You're swamped, running around like a crazy person, and you're supposed to sit down and read a book *about* time? Yep. Here's the thing. I promise that if you finish this book, and even apply three of my strat-egies to avoid the real time traps of life, you'll be able to count the moments it took to read it as *time saved*.

Your Protest:
I don't have TIME to read this book about time!
My Promise:
Read it and it will SAVE you time!

We'll get to my story in a moment. Maybe. If you have time. If you're really in a rush, simply look at the time-trap categories below, which are based on my national survey of three hundred women, and ask yourself this: which group best describes me?

► The Overwhelmed—I feel out of control most of the time.

▶ The Procrastinators—Time management? I'll think about it later.

▶ The Pressured—Everyone else is putting time pressures on me!

▶ The Self-Stressed—I am my biggest problem in managing time.

▶ The Balanced—Congratulations! We're coming to you for help.

Or if you're not quite sure, visit www.carolyncastleberry.com and answer nine simple questions in our Time Use Group Classification Tool. We'll calculate the results for you in a few seconds.

Fast Forward

Time Management Emergency?

1. **Determine which group best describes you.**

2. **Need help? Go to www.carolyncastleberry.com.**

3. **Answer nine questions under Time Use Group Classification Tool.**

4. **Determine your specific time-trap classification.**

5. **Refer to Ten + Ten = Time (see chapters 3 to 6) to immediately apply strategies for your unique needs!**

Since I can best relate to the flat-out discouraged, altogether-drained Overwhelmed—I've listed my personal top-ten strategies in chapter 3. Then I have ten more smart strategies in each of chapters 4 to 6, which focus on the other time challenges. But because each of us is different—and because we certainly will shift between the categories depending on age, whether we work at home or out in the world, and oh yeah, if we are raising little ones—it's up to you to find and create your own top-ten-current-favorites list. I've added other, multi-point strategies and questions throughout part two, Ten+Ten=Time, to give you even more ideas. Use page 236 to write down your notes for an overall Personal Time Strategy; and even while you read through this book, start applying these steps to your own life, one at a time. Watch how you are literally able to find moments, hours, dare I say *days* (!) for the things you love. Time is our greatest asset on this earth. Together, let's invest it wisely.

PART ONE

Get Ready to Take Back Time

1

Time Crunched

There is a time for everything, and a season
for every activity under heaven.

—ECCLESIASTES 3:1 NIV

As a young woman, I took time for granted. Not anymore. Some of us understand intuitively that time is our greatest gift—ours to invest for a lifetime. For others, like me, it takes a defining moment to realize that moments, hours, and days are all we have—a defining moment followed by a complete shift in life priorities. It may be losing a loved one. It may be giving up on a dream. For me it was having two healthy babies and losing two babies, one in the second trimester of pregnancy. For years I had been a career woman and wasn't even sure I had time for kids. Time was all about me. But having and losing children—struggling for the dream of motherhood I hadn't even realized was hidden deep within me—caused me to reevaluate my time in a big way. More on my story in a moment . . . as we say on TV.

First let's talk about you. After all, it's about time. Yours. In decades of television and radio interviews, I've heard one consistent theme: American women are in a time crisis. "There's just not enough time," everyone seems to say. We're doing more but are less satisfied. Fueled by both internal and external pressures, we run from task to task without pausing to ask ourselves, *Do I really want to do all this stuff? Am I investing my life where it matters?* How do we manage to find the time to balance our supercharged, oversched-uled lives?

To prove that I wasn't just imagining this time crisis, I commissioned a national survey on women and time (go to www .carolyncastleberry.com for the full scoop on how we put this together, who we interviewed, and verbatim comments from our participants). Sure enough, in an online survey of three hundred women, we found that 74 percent of them weren't happy with how they spent their time. That's three out of four!

Half of our group felt busier than they did five years ago (50 percent); nearly that many didn't feel there was enough time to get everything done (45 percent) and said they didn't have enough time for themselves (43 percent). Here's another finding that confirmed what women are saying—one in three women (34 percent) described herself as overwhelmed. Listen to what some of the women said are their greatest time traps:

> *"Too many demands on my time from people who do not consider that I have other things to do"*

> *"Too many activities at one time as a single mom"*

"Expecting too much from myself"

"Letting others tell me how things should be done"

"Lack of ambition or drive to get things done"

"I just have a lot going on. I am a full-time everything."

How Do You Feel About Your Time?

Whether or not you are also a "full-time everything," how do you feel about how you are investing your time? We asked the participants in our survey to tell us how much they agreed with several statements that measure perceptions in these four important areas impacting time management:

- ▶ Outside Pressures

- ▶ Attitudes

- ▶ Smart Strategies

- ▶ Time Wasters

The chart below shows the percentage of women who agreed strongly with each statement. Check out a couple of these statements and see if they describe you.

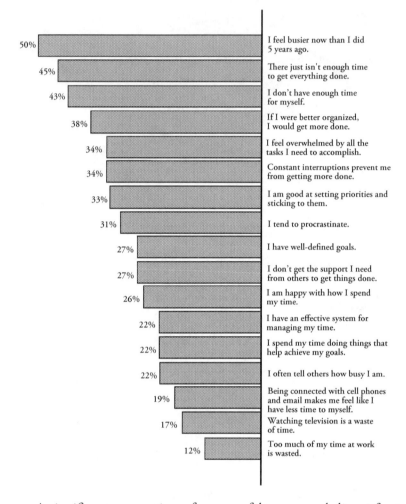

50% — I feel busier now than I did 5 years ago.

45% — There just isn't enough time to get everything done.

43% — I don't have enough time for myself.

38% — If I were better organized, I would get more done.

34% — I feel overwhelmed by all the tasks I need to accomplish.

34% — Constant interruptions prevent me from getting more done.

33% — I am good at setting priorities and sticking to them.

31% — I tend to procrastinate.

27% — I have well-defined goals.

27% — I don't get the support I need from others to get things done.

26% — I am happy with how I spend my time.

22% — I have an effective system for managing my time.

22% — I spend my time doing things that help achieve my goals.

22% — I often tell others how busy I am.

19% — Being connected with cell phones and email makes me feel like I have less time to myself.

17% — Watching television is a waste of time.

12% — Too much of my time at work is wasted.

A significant proportion of women felt stress and dissatisfaction about time management, as shown by the large percentages agreeing strongly with the top three statements in this chart. Based on these attitudes toward time, we identified five groups of women, each with distinctive characteristics. Chances are you'll see yourself in one of these "time groups"—which range from women who felt overwhelmed when it came to time management (34 percent) all the way to those who were very organized and comfortable with their ability to effectively use their time (26 percent). The remaining 40 percent felt they needed some help in managing time and had specific challenges that keep them from doing so.

If you're looking for your basic, how-to-do-more-stuff time-management book, this isn't it. Instead, we'll look at the real *reasons* we're not investing our time the way we want to. You'll be able to identify the traps that are robbing you of your greatest asset. But here's the big difference between this book and many others: in these pages, we'll go way beyond simple strategies for time management because our results showed that a woman's relationship with time isn't determined by *what* she does or *how much* she is able to accomplish. Rather it's determined by *how she feels* about what she does. It involves your own relationship with time—your personal scale of balance—which is unique to you and is directly related to this key question: are you investing your life where it matters *to you*?

> A woman's relationship with time isn't determined by what she does or how much she is able to it accomplish. Rather it's determined by how she feels about what she does.

That's why this book won't focus on checking off more items on your to-do list. (Who needs that?) We won't be trying to get more done. (Oh, doesn't that feel good?!) In fact, in some cases you may find that the key to healthy time investment is doing less! (That's me.)

What Do We Want Anyway?

Interestingly, only one in four women had a clear idea of what really mattered to her and how to achieve it; in other words, goals. Only 22 percent of the women we surveyed felt they had an effective system for managing time, and only 27 percent had well-defined goals. That's close to the number that reported being happy with how they were investing their time on this earth. These are the women we call our Balanced Group, and we'll learn a great deal from them.

We also found that women fit into four other basic categories: the Overwhelmed (put me here for much of my life), the Procrastinators, the Pressured, and the Self-Stressed.

You Know Who You Are

The good news is there are solutions for all these groups, even if it's one baby step at a time. And my guess is that when you look at the list—Overwhelmed, Procrastinators, Pressured, and Self-Stressed—you intuitively know where you fit. Something inside tells us that somebody is causing all these time pressures or, dare I say, that we are the problem in our own lives. First, let's visit the four segments of women we found in our survey. Later in the book we'll address specific strategies to take back time for all of them.

The Overwhelmed

Women in this first group typically answer to the label of either Superwoman or Single Mom. Here are some more of their cries for help:

> *"I have entirely too much stress because I don't seem to have enough time and money to invest either one properly."*

"I am not disciplined enough to stay on task; too many uncontrollable things demand my time . . . mainly my nine children!"

"I have too much on my plate at once."

Oh boy, I can relate! We may not have nine children (God bless you, dear soul!), but most of us have way too much on our plates at once. The Overwhelmed are the ones who feel the most unbalanced and out of control when it comes to time management. These women believe they have no time for themselves and that time pressures are constantly accelerating. They believe they cannot exercise control over their time. They feel helpless:

"I am unable to set goals."

"I am feeling overstressed and overwhelmed by the demands on my life. And I have a feeling of tiredness much of the time."

"I think that I feel overwhelmed by the quantity of what has to get done and when it has to get done by."

It's easy to see why many of the Overwhelmed women feel so out of control. This group tends to be younger and includes the highest number of single parents. For these women, just surviving each day appears to be the top priority. Because I was once constantly overwhelmed, my first ten strategies to take back time will begin with you, my friends (see chapter 3). Plus, I'll throw in a bonus ten, because we need them so badly.

The Procrastinators

The second group we identified is the Procrastinators. Thirty-one percent of the women we interviewed said they had this tendency. You know her. Maybe she's you. Maybe she's me, as I glance away from my computer screen to a little clutter pile growing on my desk. I'll get to that later. Our well-intentioned Procrastinator makes big plans, has big ideas, and makes a big list of things to do. But something happens along the way:

> *"I procrastinate. I know something needs to be done at work (I'm self-employed) or around the house, but I will find an excuse to have a friend visit or play with my pets or grandson rather than tackle it."*

> *"I hate school but know it is important if I hope to advance in a career. In effect, procrastinating, homework, and working odd shifts prevent me from managing my time better."*

> *"I hate to grocery-shop, always putting it off until there is nothing in the house to eat."*

> *"I am lazy or there are just too many things going on at the same time."*

I love their honest answers. One woman summed up her life in two words: *bad habits.* Whatever the underlying reason for their lack of motivation, these women had acquired some behaviors that were literally killing their time. Our top-ten smart strategies for our Procrastinator girlfriends (see chapter 4) will target time-stealing habits.

The Pressured

Working moms, this might be you. That includes stay-at-home moms who may also home school their kids and who are working harder than anyone can imagine. You want to talk about pressure? A producer I work with was caught in the "sandwich generation," and at one point her elderly father, two grandchildren, and the children's mother who was recently divorced all lived with her. Could you keep up with that? At times, she couldn't either! Students, career women, you can certainly relate to feeling pressured too. This third group tends to be largely married with children and feels weighed down by external forces:

"People have no idea of all I'm supposed to do."

"Everyone assumes I can do it, since I've done it before."

"My friends call me, day or night, even though they know I'm working."

"If I don't do everything my kids ask of me, I think they won't feel loved or cared for."

"I stay at home with my daughter, who is eight months old, and she is very hands-on at this stage in her life . . . my entire day is spent just taking care of her.

Thirty-four percent of the women we surveyed felt that constant interruptions prevented them from getting more done, and they felt they didn't get the support they need from others (27 percent). Overall, these women felt they were not very good at making decisions on managing their time. In fact, they didn't feel empowered to make these decisions and blamed external forces for the problems. A typical attitude of this group can be summed up in this quote: "If it weren't for everyone else, I'd be fine." Hey, who hasn't felt that way!

Not surprisingly, these women said they spent the least time relaxing.

Also, many of the youngest women in our survey said they felt the most pressured. As a result, they placed a higher priority on work and career than any other group. One woman wrote, "To the extent that it lies in my own hands, I think I manage my time very well. However, as I said before, my employer pretty much 'owns' me. I have a management-level job, which we need in order to stay afloat financially, so I put in however many hours I can." Your top-ten strategies are in chapter 5.

The Self-Stressed

My friend, Tanya, is a real estate agent who is consistently the number one performer in her office. She also manages a home, raises two children, and volunteers for church and school functions, usually serving as a committee chairperson. From the outside it looks like the perfect life, doesn't it? There's just one problem—Tanya doesn't have time for all of this stuff, and the stress is chipping away at her joy with each new task she adds to her Day-Timer. Meet our fourth group of women: the Self-Stressed. These women are similar to the Pressured except for one important difference. While the Pressured woman tends to blame others for her inability to manage time, the Self-Stressed woman puts the blame right smack on herself. She may feel a need to be perfect and live up to the world's expectations, like the lady who wrote that "I am trying to accomplish too much at once." When it comes to time management, the Self-Stressed woman tends to target her own lack of organization rather than fault interruptions or a lack of support from others. One woman wrote, "I think it's a lack of discipline in this area, first of all, and I also think there are distractions that I allow to get me off track or off schedule."

This group's tendency to blame themselves may also be related to their age and general lack of life experience (the women in this group tend to be the youngest in our survey). Here are a few more of their comments:

"If I were only better at managing time, I'd be fine."

"I'm completely disorganized and under a lot of stress."

"There's not enough time in the day."

"I can't possibly cover everything on my list, so I ignore it."

Are you listening to the words? Mostly negative. These also seem to be the women who struggle with disempowering thoughts and beat themselves up on a regular basis. Have you ever been there in your life? Many of us have. That's why our ten smart strategies for the Self-Stressed (see chapter 6) will focus on thoughts and words that can help in overcoming time traps.

The Balanced

Ah . . . our heroines. The Balanced felt very in control of their time and felt generally good about their lives. Don't be jealous! This group gives us hope. They generally didn't let external factors derail their schedules. They also felt they could control their own actions with respect to time management. They were basically happy with how they spent their time. Not surprisingly, this group tended to be the oldest, and they were the least likely to have children in the house. Probably due to their age and experience, this group also felt the most satisfied with life:

> *"I prioritize what needs to be done and then prioritize what I want to do."*

> *"I simply make a plan in the morning and follow the plan."*

> *"I manage my time well."*

> *"I don't make an unrealistic schedule, because I know things in my house don't run smoothly. I basically just go with the flow of things."*

> *"I make a list of all the things that need to be done for the day and the time it will take to get them done. As each item is accomplished, it is crossed off the list."*

One survey respondent said, "Save enough time in each day/week, etc., so that there is no need to have to manage your time. There will always be free time in every day/week if you set aside time in each day that is not scheduled for anything."

I love it! We can all do that! And we don't have to wait until we're seniors to enter this arena.

Time Groups at a Glance

Here's an overview of all five of these groups, plus their basic time management needs as reflected in their comments:

GROUP	KEY ATTITUDES	DISTINGUISHING CHARACTERISTICS	SELF-EXPRESSED TIME MANAGEMENT NEEDS
Overwhelmed	» overwhelmed by external time pressures » don't know how to manage stress	» very unbalanced » often younger (18–35) » highest proportion of single mothers » highest proportion of mothers without a child-care solution	» basic management skills » possibly counseling on basic life skills
Procrastinators	» have ability to manage but are easily distracted by other activities they deem more interesting	» know what they want, but just can't seem to get there » often older (35+) » most have no children at home	» development of motivation to stick to the task at hand
Pressured	» blame external factors for inability to manage time » feel they're in control of themselves	» often younger » largest proportion of minority women » less concerned than other groups about forming relationships	» how to more effectively deal with perceived external disruptions » learning to set boundaries in relationships
Self-Stressed	» blame themselves for inability to manage time effectively	» tend to be the youngest group (18–35)	» need help in developing systems to better manage their schedules and self-perception
Balanced	» in control of internal and external factors	» very balanced » often the oldest among those surveyed (35+)	» none

You may be the hyperbusy woman who needs more time for herself and her family or the type of personality prone to daydreaming, struggling with fears, or becoming paralyzed by indecision. No matter how you describe yourself—in one or several of these categories—we are a society that is wasting time despite our busyness. We find ourselves speeding from here to there in a never-ending sequence of "important" activities, and our world is moving so fast it's hard to keep track of the days, weeks, and years anymore.

The older we get, the more we feel we just blinked and thirty years went by. So many valuable moments are gone—time that we'll never, ever get back. With all the responsibilities we have to face each day in our work, families, and personal lives, we must first learn to get control of our time—this limited resource—and our greatest God-given asset here on this earth.

Back to my story. As I mentioned, having children for me was extremely difficult, and our first pregnancy ended in a miscarriage. We had planned to visit my husband's family the following week for a get-together when I told him, "John, I can't go. I can't speak to anyone. I need to go away by myself for a while." Poor John. He didn't know what to think. He had just lost a baby too, and now I was going away to think and pray. How was he going to explain this to his family? But I was so absorbed in my own pain that all I could think of was escape. Refuge.

I found it in a place called Safety Harbor in Tampa, recommended by a friend. I loved this quiet resort getaway by still waters. But it was also a place for families and friends, and it seemed like I was the only one who came alone. Ate alone. Walked alone. When people asked me if I was okay, I decided to be honest and said, "I just lost a baby, and I need some time." And the people responded in a wonderful way. I'll always be grateful for their understanding and kindness to me.

But there was another Person I had to make peace with. The Lord. The Lord of my life, the Lord of my future, the Lord of all time. "God, how could this happen? Why is life so unfair? Why did you give us this baby in the first place just to lose her?" I had already named her Chloe. I just knew she was a girl. "Lord, everything that was so important in life just doesn't seem to matter anymore." I was so angry with God, I didn't hesitate to tell him about it. Then I slept. Then I gave him another earful and slept some more.

During that last day of pouring out my hurt, lost dreams, confusion, and anger to the Lord, I suddenly felt his presence. I felt peace. Above all, I felt his love and his Spirit whispering to my spirit, *Carolyn, I love you and haven't left you. I still have wonderful plans for you and John. Loss is just a part of life. Will you love me anyway?*

In that moment, through my tears, I said, "Yes, I will love you. Yes, I believe you. Yes, I will surrender to you—even this desire to be a mom. If it never happens, I will love you anyway."

I went back home, and in the years to come, John and I would go on to have a beautiful baby girl we named Lindsay. We would also feel the devastating pain of losing another baby, a boy, in the second trimester of pregnancy. His name was David. We then had another beautiful baby girl we named Brooke, and John's son from a previous marriage came to live with us at age twelve. Jack, my stepson, rounded out our family. Yes, indeed, the Lord had plans.

Perhaps it was our loss and hardship in having children that caused me to fall so deeply in love with my babies. Perhaps this newscaster found her heart for the first time. Perhaps it's just the miracle of children, but I knew I had to spend as much time with my kids as possible. With sudden clarity, I knew this was what I was put on earth to do.

There was just one problem. Money. Talk about crashing down to earth with a huge dose of reality. Just as our first baby was born, John and I faced a devastating financial crisis. Downsizing is a word we both know well in the tumultuous world of broadcasting (John is a sportscaster), and since I had planned to quit my job as a reporter, we were looking at an income of zero. We had to change those plans, and I went back to a job of reporting bad news.

As I've written in two business books, John and I now know how to make life work, no matter what the circumstances, and I teach women around the world that they always have choices. Hey, now I get to report good news, like writing this for you! But back then, as a young couple, we didn't know what to do. I just knew that I wanted more time for my babies but could never scrape more together. I thought time would always be there, that there would be days ahead where I could modify my schedule, but I was discovering my days were not my own. That realization became most poignant when one of Lindsay's first words to me turned out to be "bye-bye" as I raced to another news story.

I realized that time was all I had while my children were little, and I became determined to spend as much of it with my family as I could.

The editors I've worked with over the years are much smarter than I am. Thomas Womack, a sharp and insightful editor, realized that in writing books about money, I was really writing about time— what I call our greatest asset and a much more valuable currency. I had been a wage slave and my freedom to choose how I spend my time came through none other than Jesus Christ. Really. His wisdom and guidance showed me how to walk in true freedom.

My heart was with my family, but much of my time still belonged to my career. That's when I made the choice to walk away from a job I'd held for fourteen years as a local newscaster. I had a no-compete clause in my contract that prohibited me from working in any capacity at another local station for one year. I couldn't anchor, report, make coffee, or even step foot in the building to serve as the janitor at another station for 365 days.

Ah . . . time. As I've written about in *Women, Take Charge of Your Money* and *Women, Get Answers About Your Money,* it was God's wisdom in showing me how to invest money wisely that allowed me the choice and the dignity to walk away from a job that stressed my spirit daily and stole my family time.

It was one of those periods of life when I also heard that challenging voice of the Lord saying, *Move on. I have something better for you. Trust me.* Now, I haven't always been a person of great faith who knows the right thing to do and actually does it. Many times worry and practical responsibilities get the best of me—after all, I have little mouths to feed! But for some reason this time I actually had the faith to do the right thing. In deciding to walk away from a safe and secure job as a reporter (reporting mostly bad news), I held on to to Galatians 5:1: "It was for freedom that Christ set us free; therefore keep standing firm and do not be subject again to a yoke of slavery" (NASB). As a "wage slave," I made the decision to grasp freedom, walk away, and give myself the gift of time to think.

During my days off, I was faced with many choices. Many of my resulting decisions were good—they just weren't the best. Therefore they weren't God's will for my life. One day during this confusing time, I lay on the floor, facedown in prayer, and said, "Lord,

> *It was for freedom that Christ set us free; therefore keep standing firm and do not be subject again to a yoke of slavery.*
>
> —*Galatians 5:1 NASB*

I'm so sick and tired of asking you to get on board with my plans. This time I want to get on board with *your* plans. What is it that you require of this life?"

That very day I got an answer. A producer from the Christian Broadcasting Network called to tell me about a show called *Living the Life* that reaches out to women. A week later God set me on a path of reporting and writing books about the good news of Christ—something this newscaster, who had made a life of reporting bad news, had only dreamed of doing. And my greatest dream—more hours with my little family; a new path; and a better investment of my greatest asset, time—came true.

> "But one never gets the feeling when studying the life of Christ that He ever hurried, that He ever had to play 'catch up,' or that He was ever taken by surprise."
>
> —*Gordon MacDonald,*
> Ordering Your Private World

The test of time. Where are your time traps? How will you invest the years you have on this earth? Our first step in solving this problem is tracking where our time goes. That may take more than a moment. But even Jesus stepped away from the crowds who followed him everywhere so he could take time to rest, regroup, and communicate with the Father.

The Master of Time

In *Ordering Your Private World*, Gordon MacDonald asks whether we are driven or called when we invest our time. For example, are we driven by our need to succeed? Are we feeling overly responsible for areas in life that aren't our responsibility? Or are we called by the Father of time into a life of purpose and clarity?

The good news is that we have someone to learn from in managing our most valuable asset—the Lord of time, Jesus, who never seemed to waste a minute. He never lost focus.

As MacDonald observes,

When I look into the Bible, I am deeply impressed with the practical lessons on organization that one can learn from the life and work of Jesus Christ. All four Gospel writers present to us a picture of Jesus under constant pressure, as He was pursued by friend and enemy alike. His every word was monitored, every action was analyzed, every gesture was commented upon.[1]

Talk about pressure! But through it all, Jesus had a firm handle on time. He was clear on his purpose and even took private time with the Father so he could regain his strength as the crowds followed him everywhere. He took time to speak with people whom many of us would pass on the street. Jesus wasn't in a hurry, even though he had an urgent mission and only thirty-three years to complete it. Thank God he didn't procrastinate!

As we learn in these pages to be better stewards of our time, I'll take us back to the Bible many times—because on this topic, as with every other area of life, it provides words of hope that go beyond just good information. God provides power to change your investment of time, if you ask him. The first step is determining the leaks in your time budget. Who and what is stealing your time without your permission?

ACTION APPLICATION

Track Your Time

Are the areas in which you're investing your time really that important to you, or have you been lured into giving away your greatest asset to anyone and everyone without a thought?

Are you investing yourself where it matters to you?

Here's a simple but valuable exercise. Turn to the Where Does the Time Go? log on page 235. Track your time to see how you use it—keep a daily log of how much time goes to each activity you're involved in. A few minutes of writing and analyzing these logs can show you much more clearly how to eliminate many hours of wasted time. You'll see how much time is spent in unexpected ways, whether from internal or external time stealers. Often it appears that the busier you feel, the more time you waste. Another important discovery you will make is how much time things really take. One of the most common problems in personal time management is underestimating the time needed for each activity.

So take a few days or a week, and write down what you do with your time, just as you would log your spending if you're setting up a budget or a log of your calorie intake if you're embarking on a diet. If you're like me, chances are you'll be surprised at where the time goes.

2

This Is Your Time

"I know the plans I have for you," announces the Lord.
"I want you to enjoy success. I do not plan to harm you.
I will give you hope for the years to come."

—JEREMIAH 29:11 NLRV

W ho hasn't said, "Where does the time go?" If you completed the Action Application in chapter 1, you may be stunned at where you are spending or wasting your time. Don't be discouraged. This is wonderful! This is a fantastic beginning because you are starting to open your eyes. In my financial reports I always say that taking charge of your money begins by understanding what's coming in and what's going out. You know that dreaded word *budget*. The same is true when it comes to managing your time. Is it true that we really don't have enough time? Or has God given us everything we need to accomplish his purposes? The Irish have a proverb: "When God made time, he made a lot of it." Can this be true? Is it possible that God has given us everything we need, including enough time?

"When God made time, he made a lot of it."

—Irish proverb

Let's break it down. We know we have twenty-four hours in a day, but exactly where are we investing these precious moments? Here's a place to start: in his article, "The Dash Between the Dates,"[1] Jackson Snyder wrote that he put together a list of things we do and how much time is consumed by these activities over a seventy-five-year lifespan. Typically, we spend:

- twenty-four years sleeping

- twenty-four years working

- six years dressing

- four years waiting in line

- eight months on the telephone

- six months tying shoes

- three months signing checks/paying bills

Also, consider how we waste time emotionally. Snyder claims that worry and anger top the list of time-wasting activities. For example, he challenges us to count how many years we've wasted in bitterness and resentment. How many years have escaped us because of procrastination, indecision, complaining, or self-pity? When we get focused on these emotional hang-ups, the God-given lives we were meant to live pass right on by.

Time and Your Priorities

In our study, we asked women to report how many hours per week, on average, they spent doing various activities. Check out the chart below:

Average Number of Hours Spent per Week

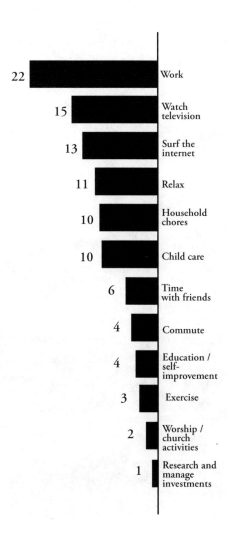

The totals for these activities can be categorized into these four groups:

- *Recreation.* This included such activities as watching television, surfing the web, relaxing, and spending time with friends and averaged forty-five hours per week.

- *Work and commuting.* These activities took an average of twenty-six hours a week for these women. (Note that this average includes women who don't work outside the home.)

- *Child care and household chores.* This category takes into account all domestic responsibilities and totaled twenty hours per week.

- *Well-being.* Activites such as exercise, education and self-improvement, worship and church activities, and researching and managing financial investments totaled ten hours per week.

How closely does your own use of time in a typical week match these figures? More important, how closely do you think your time-spending fits with your own true priorities? Are you investing time where it matters to you?

Who Determines Your Priorities?

Consider Maura, a veterinarian. An Overwhelmed, Self-Stressed woman who can understand feeling Pressured and trying to live up to the world's standard of perfection. She had studied for eight years to become a doctor, then worked for another ten years building a solid business and reputation. By the world's standards she did everything right; she had lots of money and all of the trappings of success. But she still couldn't shake the emptiness she felt in her heart.

She and her family paid a high price in terms of time. Maura told me, "So much of the day was running. Running between appointments and surgery. There were days I would go in at eight in the morning and leave at ten at night." She worked seventy to eighty hours per week, and it was beginning to take its toll on her health. When she became pregnant, she knew this high-powered, high-stress lifestyle wouldn't bring true happiness.

One day in her office, she hit the wall. She had an epiphany of sorts as she remembered hearing about a person who could change everything. A person who had paid the ultimate price—his life—so she could experience a life that was abundant and eternal. All alone, she prayed a simple prayer inviting Jesus Christ to become her personal Lord and Savior and Lord of her time.

Fireworks didn't go off. Life didn't change overnight. Instead, she began to learn a different way to take charge of her time—choosing work that put her family first and scaling back on her frenetic work life. Maura says she has a new set of time priorities now, "Because what pleases God is our faith, and if we can see where we are going, and we can do it on our own strength, we don't need him. And that's not where God wants us to be. He wants us to be in a place where we are doing even bigger things, way bigger than what we can do on our own."

For Maura, those bigger things meant littler things, like picking up her kids from school, helping with homework. Just being there.

What Matters Anyway?

Maura's story brings up the critical issue of priorities—an inescapable topic when it comes to evaluating and refining our time management. Are you doing what really matters to you? When asked to rank their priorities for investing time, the women in our survey placed the highest priority on caring for loved ones, followed by building relationships. Not surprisingly, exercise and managing investments were the two lowest priorities among the items tested. After all, we forget about taking care of ourselves or even thinking about our futures in our overscheduled lives.

Priorities

#1 **Caring for children and loved ones**

#2 **Building relationships**

#3 **Work / career**

#4 **Relaxation**

#5 **Education / self-improvement**

#6 **Recreation / entertainment**

#7 **Worship / church activities**

#8 **Exercise**

#9 **Money making / investing**

The survey results clearly show that women across most time groups value those activities that allow them to connect with others. "Caring for children and loved ones" was ranked first by 40 percent of the survey participants (more than twice as often as any other activity), and 63 percent listed it as one of their top three. Meanwhile, both "building relationships" and "work / career" were top-three choices by just under half of the women.

The table below shows the average rankings for each of the categories we've identified. It's noteworthy that the Pressured—the group that feels others are responsible for creating their time pressures—place a relatively lower value on relationship building than other groups. Can you blame them? It's all about time, and they feel others are stealing theirs. Like these women:

> *"Right now, I am interrupted by my two children who constantly need my attention."*

> *"I may be in the full swing of things and someone calls. I do have a hands-free phone, but I hate to wear it while doing what I need to do. And I do not want to be rude, but sometimes I just say, 'come on over.' I have a lot going on at home."*

> *"I have constant interruptions."*

> *"My grandchildren constantly need me to be there."*

Time Priorities

OVERWHELMED	PROCRASTINATORS	PRESSURED	SELF-STRESSED	BALANCED
1. Caring for children and loved ones	1. Caring for children and loved ones	1. Caring for children and loved ones	1. Caring for children and loved ones	1. Caring for children and loved ones
2. Building relationships	2. Building relationships	2. Work / career	2. Work / career	2. Building relationships
3. Work / career	3. Relaxation	3. Relaxation	3. Building relationships	3. Work / career
4. Relaxation	4. Work / career	4. Building relationships	4. Education / self-improvement	4. Relaxation
5. Education / self-improvement	5. Recreation / entertainment	5. Education / self-improvement	5. Worship / church activities	5. Education / self-improvement
6. Recreation / entertainment	6. Worship / church activities	6. Worship / church activities	6. Relaxation	6. Recreation / entertainment
7. Exercise	7. Education / self-improvement	7. Exercise	7. Recreation / entertainment	7. Worship / church activities
8. Worship / church activities	8. Exercise	8. Recreation / entertainment	8. Money making / investing	8. Exercise
9. Money making / investing	9. Money making / investing	9. Money making / investing	9. Exercise	9. Money making/ investing

Top Time Factors

Okay, since the women brought it up, let's talk about kids. You've heard the expression—"children will change your life"? Sure enough. And they will definitely impact your time priorities. The biggest change, once a woman has a child, is that every other priority shifts down on the list. Not surprising. One woman said other priorities completely got the boot: "I always have to stop what I am doing and tend to the kids, or the phone, or the door. It's very exasperating." Exasperating though it is sometimes, caring for loved ones is most important to women between ages twenty-five and fifty-four—prime years for starting and raising a family. And as our population ages, many women find they have to care for their parents after their children leave home!

Age also matters, giving us both hope and a time reality-check, depending upon family and finances. One older woman said her time is spent in a way she never planned for: "A grandchild lives with us and we support him. We love him and wouldn't change things." Another senior writes, "I would love to be retired and get done the things I need to do. Unfortunately, I have to work to make a living."

However, our research found that for many women the importance of work and career declines steadily as they age, while the importance of both relaxation and worship increase. Listen to this beacon of hope for the rest of us: "There is nothing I could do better. I choose to have a very slow, easy, laid-back schedule. I enjoy the path. It is a nice, slow, easy enjoyable journey." Ah . . . a nap, anyone? Sadly, the youngest women in the research placed the lowest importance on relaxation and worship, while women over age sixty-five placed the greatest importance on them.

The Bottom Line

These are just a couple of the factors that impact your time priorities. For the full report go to www.carolyncastleberry.com. But here's the bottom line: three out of four women wanted to make an improvement in managing their time. This means that what we want to do—what's truly important to us—isn't what we're actually doing. For example, many working moms wanted to spend more time with their children but couldn't, due to time constraints. That was me, as well.

Three out of four women wanted to make an improvement in managing their time.

Okay, we've been tracking our time using the Where Does the Time Go? log, giving us an indication of where it's all going. We've discussed our priorities and asked if you are doing what you want to do with your life, and if not, why not? Now you are about to complete an exercise that will enable you to weigh your priorities. Then on to our next step. Of course, I recommend reading this book cover to cover. Hey, I wrote it—what do you expect me to say? But I know you're busy, and for time's sake, you may want to skip to the time trap that is calling your name in Ten + Ten = Time (chapters 3–6):

▸ Hello, Overwhelmed. Chapter 3 gives you my top ten strategies to take back time, plus ten more minor tips. See page 43!

▸ Miss Procrastinator, let's nail those time-stealing habits before they nail you. Ten smart strategies in chapter 4 will get you started today. Not tomorrow. Skip to page 71.

▸ Don't feel Pressured anymore, my friends. Ten smart strategies for stellar decision making await your review in chapter 5, starting on page 104.

▸ Ah, the Self-Stressed. Be very kind to yourself as you consider ten smart strategies for avoiding time traps through thoughts and words in chapter 6. Think about turning to page 129.

Finally, we'll take a good look at the time traps and best investments of time in what most of you say are your top priorities: relationships and work that matters (whether it's a career in or out of the home). Part three, Investing Time and Talents, will tackle one of your least favorite (most fear-inducing) priorities: money. Sorry, ladies, it's important. Someone recently asked me, "What does money have to do with time?" My answer? "Everything!" Until you are able to get a handle on fear in this area of life, in submission to God, you will never truly own your time.

Lest you think I consider myself some sort of time guru, let me tell you how much I struggle with making wise decisions. While writing this book, I made one of the dumbest time mistakes ever. I took a speaking job on a cruise without checking the school calendar for my kids. After making the commitment, my littlest one informed me that she was going to be in her first-ever school play—*The Music Man*. She was so excited because she was part of the quartet (yes, it was an all-girls quartet), and she couldn't wait to read and sing me her part. Do you see where I'm going? That play turned out to be on the very days I had committed to travel. I missed opening night. I missed closing night. Granted, I went to as many play rehearsals as I possibly could, but it wasn't the same. I missed it because of bad time management. The Self-Stressed lady in me wouldn't let me hear the end of it.

Here's the thing. We will never completely master time or its management, but we can do better. We can become aware of and overcome the real time traps in our lives that steal our hours and days. We can invest time according to our priorities. When we make bad time decisions, like I have, we'll know how to correct this in the future. This is our time! *Note to Carolyn: always check the school calendar before committing to anything.*

ACTION APPLICATION

What Matters to You?

Here's an interesting test we came up with while doing our survey. In determining your own priorities, how would you change the amount of time you spend doing each of the following activities to increase your sense of well-being? (Place a check in the appropriate column for each activity. All that matters here is whether you want to *change* how much time you're spending in this activity—regardless of whether that means more time or less time.)

ACTIVITY	(A) LEAVE ABOUT THE SAME	(B) CHANGE A LITTLE	(C) CHANGE A LOT
working			
commuting			
watching television			
household chores			
child care			
exercising			
surfing the internet			
being with friends			
relaxing			
education / self-improvement			
researching and managing investments			
worship / church activities			

ACTION APPLICATION

Now give yourself zero points for each check in column A, one point for each check in column B, and four points for each check in column C. Add these up to get your score.

Below is the "balance category" you belong to, depending on your score:

0 to 6—Balanced

7 to 12—Doing well

13 to 18—Doing okay, but could improve

19 to 24—Slipping out of control

25 to 36—Out of control

37 or higher—In serious trouble (Don't worry. It's about time for a change.)

PART TWO

Ten + Ten = Time

3

The Overwhelmed

10 Smart Strategies to Tame Time Traps

Steep your life in God-reality, God-initiative, God-provisions.
Don't worry about missing out.
You'll find all your everyday human concerns will be met.

—MATTHEW 6:33 MSG

Ten + Ten = Time

Strategies to Tame Time Traps

Strategy #1: Meet with God First.

Strategy #2: Write Your Mission Statement.

Strategy #3: Juggle One Ball at a Time.

Strategy #4: Create Flexible Goals.

Strategy #5: Plan Each Day.

Strategy #6: Schedule Unscheduled Time.

Strategy #7: Delegate, Delegate, Delegate.

Strategy #8: Unclutter Your Life.

Strategy #9: Really Rest.

Strategy #10: Reflect.

A NOTE FROM GOD

My Dear Overwhelmed Daughter:

On those days when you feel beyond exhausted, weary and heavy-laden, come to me. Take a break with me and recover your strength and joy. On those days when you feel that no one understands, come to me. I am tender and humble in heart and you will find rest for your soul. On those days when you feel weighed down by all of your responsibilities, come to me. I will renew your focus and give you peace that passes all comprehension. On those days when you feel that it's all just too much, come to me. Know that I have promised never to leave or forsake you. You can do all things through my power, by my strength and for my glory.

Love always,
God

(From Matthew 11:28–29; Habakkuk 3:17–19; Philippians 4:6–13)

Hooray for Superwoman! She does everything herself, never asking for help and never complaining. She cleans up after her family, cooks their meals, and does their laundry. She answers the phone, bakes for the bake sale, and tries to pay the bills.

But it doesn't stop there. She's also a real-estate agent who tells her clients, "Call me anytime if you have any problems or questions." So her cell phone rings constantly. She doesn't enjoy dinner because she's interrupted a dozen times. After dinner, the dog needs to be walked, but the kids are too busy trying to break the code of the latest Nintendo game. So she walks the dog and takes along her cell phone so she can have "private time" to talk to her clients in peace.

When she's back home, she supervises the kids' finishing their homework, their chores, and their baths. Once they're off to bed, she gets their clothes and lunches ready for the next school day. At eleven o'clock she finally goes to bed, thinking about the three houses she has to show the next day as well as her closing appointment. Plus she just signed on a new client who needs to move within the next two months.

After a night filled with busy dreams, her alarm goes off at 5:00 a.m. so she can get herself ready before anyone else is up. She wakes the kids, makes breakfast for everyone, gets the kids dressed, and takes them to school. This afternoon, once she's home from all her appointments, she'll need to pick up the kids and start the madness all over again. Whew!

Many of us love to play the role of Superwoman. But while her accomplishments might sound impressive, let's take a peek under the surface at her darker side. This woman takes all the responsibilities upon herself because she doesn't trust others enough to do what they're more than capable of doing. And since she never delegates or asks for help, she burns out quickly. She has no clue where her days and weeks and months have gone. She can't remember the last time she took a vacation, and when she did, she was still taking calls from her clients, taking care of the kids, and trying to please everyone— everyone except herself. Although she enjoys her job immensely and loves her family dearly, she feels empty, overwhelmed, and exhausted. And she has no idea where the time—where her life—has gone. Sound familiar?

Meet Miss Overwhelmed. While this scenario sounds hopeless, I'm here to tell you that this wacky, well-intentioned, out-of-control life you've been living is about to change. Hope begins by first opening your eyes and then focusing on what's really important to you and what can be cut from your life.

It also means learning everyday strategies to help you. Baby steps, if you will. The nuts and bolts of time management. As I promised, we won't stay here. But let's take a moment to reflect again on the good news for all of us that comes from the Balanced respondents—those who say they're generally happy with how they're spending time—before we confront our personal time stealers. Listen to some of their comments when we asked them to share their best solutions for managing time:

> *"I get up early enough to be able to start my day in a positive manner. Since I do have health problems that I must consider, I plan my day around them, and I still get my things done."*

> *"I try to do the most important things that take the least amount of time first and work from there."*

> *"I set long-term goals and then take days one at a time. I prioritize the tasks for each day and plan the most efficient way to get them accomplished."*

Some combination of these three simple steps was mentioned by most of the Balanced women who have learned to successfully overcome the obstacles that keep us from wisely using our time. Adding to this, let me give you *ten strategies I've learned* over the years from my own trials and errors and from countless interviews, and echoed in the comments of our Balanced women.

Strategy #1: Meet with God First

In my books on managing money, I've stressed the importance of meeting first with my CEO—God. Just as he will multiply your money when you give it first to him, he'll also multiply your time when you put him at the top of your priority list. I know this doesn't sound logical, but it works. A psalm of David reads, "Give ear to my words, O LORD, consider my sighing. Listen to my cry for help, my King and my God, for to you I pray. In the morning, O LORD, you hear my voice; in the morning I lay my requests before you and wait in expectation" (Psalm 5:1–3 NIV).

I don't believe the Lord cares whether you meet with him in the morning or at night. He just cares that you regularly take the time to meet with him to read his Word and to pray.

---

10 Baby Steps to Balancing Time

▶ **Write goals for your life. "Know where you are headed, and you will stay on solid ground." (Proverbs 4:26 CEV)**

▶ **Learn when to say no and when to say yes.**

▶ **First thing in the morning, create a plan for the day.**

▶ **Write your top goal for the day. This is your most important priority.**

▶ **Be realistic about what can be accomplished in a given amount of time.**

> ▸ Prioritize other items on your to-do list.

> ▸ Keep a schedule that works with your personality. I use a Palm PDA and would be lost without it. My husband still has a trusty old day book with scribbles everywhere. (Hey, it works for him.)

> ▸ Schedule exercise. If you don't, it's likely you won't "just do it" at all.

> ▸ Schedule rest days. Yes, I'm serious.

> ▸ Schedule fun times with family and friends. You know what they say about all work. That means you too, stay-at-home moms!

Can't find the time, you say? I understand. When I worked in news, I'd often race off to chase the day's story without first stopping to say hello to my Friend and Savior. Invariably my day would feel like a waste of time. The biggest enemy I had to deal with was me, particularly when it came to that beloved snooze button on the alarm. You know what I mean. You keep hitting that button until the very last minute, then rush frantically around the house, usually forgetting your lunch or cell phone. But it doesn't have to be that way.

As I learned to put the Lord at the very top of my daily schedule, I began finding extra time. My days became better ordered, and I felt more focused. Now I crave that morning time with the Lord and can't imagine starting my day without it. If you choose to retain only one thing from this book, please make it this: meet daily with God—

because it will change your life by putting you in touch with his purpose and plan for your life. I spend time with him by simply reading the Bible and praying. Your time with him may be a prayer walk, devotionals, or listening to inspirational songs and teachings. Get creative, and he will multiply the time you spend with him.

> **Take a moment to consider what is keeping you from committing this time to God and what you can do to overcome that. Write it down here:**
>
>
>
> **Can't commit to a daily quiet time? Commit to one time this week and two times next week and see where it leads. Write down when and how you'll spend time with God here.**

Strategy #2: Write Your Mission Statement

Our priorities will never be perfectly implemented. And from our survey results we can see how priorities change with circumstances and age. But have you ever experienced a time in your life when everything just seemed to fall into place? Have you felt God working powerfully and knew you were doing exactly what you should be doing?

I call this being in the "God Zone." In doing a television segment with me, Dr. Barry Sears, creator of the Zone Diet, described the Zone as a place where your mind is calm and amazingly clear. Life just works. He was describing a physical and mental phenomenon. Spiritually, I've felt that I'm in the God Zone when I'm right in the middle of God's will for my life. It's when I'm clear on my God-given mission and am fully involved in reaching it—when I'm most concerned with *his* plans and purposes instead of just worrying about my own.

We all need some guidance—a road sign, if you will—to lead us to the God Zone. Proverbs 4:26 tells us, "Know where you are headed, and you will stay on solid ground" (CEV).

After spending time alone with the Lord, praying and reading his word, consider creating your own mission statement. It might just be a sentence, and that's okay. Almost every big and successful company creates and sticks to its mission statement. It helps leaders stay focused on what they're all about and what they're trying to accomplish. Your mission statement should explain what makes you unique, what principles you stand for, what makes you tick, and what you want your life to be about.

My mission statement is simple: "To love God, serve him, and speak his name at every opportunity." That pretty much covers it, personally and professionally. God is at the top of my priority list, followed by family, then everything else. One of Nike's mission statements was spelled out in two words, *Crush Reebok*. It doesn't

> *"Know where you are headed, and you will stay on solid ground."*
>
> —*Proverbs 4:26* CEV

matter how many words you use, but it is important to put something down on paper. Answer these three questions as briefly as possible:

1. *What is it that I love to do?*

2. *What brings me the most joy?*

3. *What do I absolutely know I have to do before leaving this earth?*

Now use those answers to create your own simple mission statement:

Now pray over it. Write it out and tack it on your mirror to review over the next week. Live with it and see how it feels. If you love it, if it defines who you want to be and how you think your life will count, you're on the right track. If not, refine!

There will be times in life when you have absolutely no clue what you're supposed to be doing. When you find yourself off track, for whatever reason, your mission statement will become a clarifying point to guide you back to God's plan for your life—back to the God Zone.

Strategy #3: Juggle One Ball at a Time

Someone who certainly knew how to follow in the time-investment footsteps of Christ was Mother Teresa. She knew to keep her eyes on the important things: "We are committed to feed Christ who is hungry, committed to clothe Christ who is naked, committed to take in Christ who has no home—and to do all this with a smile on our face and bursting with joy. . . . But the important thing is not to try to do everything. . . . I don't have to do everything . . . only those things pleasing to Christ."[1]

For those of us who need a time clue—there's one for us. We may not live the life of Mother Teresa, but we do know this: we don't have to do everything! God gives us permission to do one thing at a time, to respond to those opportunities he gives us as they arise; he doesn't call us to take over his job! Guess what? God is God, and we're not. How often do we need to remind ourselves just to steer our own car and not reach through the windows to the two others nearest us?

I wish I'd known these truths as a younger woman. I tell everyone that I'm still recovering from a disease called MDD—Mommy Distraction Disorder. As I mentioned, I was definitely in the Overwhelmed category when I worked as a newscaster while trying to raise a family. For years I tried to handle everything at once, while accomplishing very little. This frenetic cycle can be very frustrating. It seems like you're doing a lot at one time, but at the end of the day you feel completely unsatisfied with time spent. My friend Lisa says, "I prided myself as an ace multitasker and could certainly always get a ton done, but I felt like I didn't do any of it well. It was like I was babysitting everything from my kids to my job, caring for everything on a surface level, but never going as deep as I wanted. I gave myself a solid B+ most days, but no subject earned an A."

Guess what, ladies? Whoever told us we could have it all didn't explain that it wasn't supposed to happen all at once. We can certainly have a full and blessed life, but that takes a lifetime, not a day.

So why can't we handle everything at once?

In an article on task switching, Joshua S. Rubinstein provides some revealing answers. He explains that when people toggle between browsing the Web and using other computer programs, talk on cell phones while driving, pilot jumbo jets or monitor air traffic, they're using the executive control processes of the brain. Rubinstein gives a wake-up call as he reports that "for all types of tasks, subjects lost time when they had to switch from one task to another, and time costs increased with the complexity of the tasks, so it took significantly longer to switch between more complex tasks."[2] Multitasking sits high on the list of desired skills these days, but at what cost? The high price just might be time lost.

A juggler I interviewed brought it all back into balance and perspective by reminding me to focus on one thing at a time. Moms, are you listening? The juggler was Dan Thurmon, author of *Success in Action: The Direct Path to Your Higher Potential*. He told me that when he appears to be doing many different things all at the same time, like juggling balls, what he's actually accomplishing successfully is just one thing at a time, quickly and in the proper sequence, *focusing on one ball at a time.*

Thurmon reminded me that each of us is given 86,400 seconds in a day to spend or lose. Can you imagine if that were money? Imagine if someone deposited $86,400 into a bank account for you each morning and said it's yours to manage. I don't know about you, but I would be very careful how I saved and invested it. Yet I found myself wasting a currency that's much more valuable—my time—by trying to juggle everything at once.

As one Balanced lady put it, "I try hard to stay on task; that way I can get done what I need to do on a daily basis."

Strategy #4: Create Flexible Goals

As I mentioned, our survey showed that only 27 percent of women had well-defined goals. That means 73 percent didn't. Interestingly, that's nearly the same percentage of women (74 percent) who weren't happy with how they spent their time. It's hard to find joy and satisfaction when we have no idea what that looks like.

After you've written a mission statement, you have to put hands and feet to your aspirations—how are you actually going to accomplish your mission? What are the steps required? Like it or not, you have to set some goals. Here are three ideas to get you started:

1. For the single mom: find one friend I can rely on to babysit one night every other week. I'll watch her children on alternate weeks, giving us both a bit of personal time.

2. For the student: find a part-time job, ten hours a week, to reduce my debt load. Create a budget (and stick to it!) to begin saving $100 per month.

3. For the stay-at-home mom: join a church group of ladies to share my victories, frustrations, and, yes, sometimes loneliness. This will also be my group to exercise with by walking our kids together twice a week for one hour. If a group like this doesn't exist, I'll create one.

One Balanced lady said, "I set daily goals, yet allow flexibility for change; and reevaluate as necessary." Another wrote, "I set goals for myself each day, small ones, so I do not feel overwhelmed. I also have a disability, so I have to make sure not to push myself too hard. I set doing chores for fifteen-minute increments, make a list of things I want to accomplish, and cross them off as they get done.

That makes this daunting task much more doable, doesn't it? I admit that I used to hate goal setting. It stressed me out, and I felt that once I put my goals on paper, I had to accomplish them or I would be a failure. But the truth is we have to stay flexible in handling our goals. What we put on paper now may not be anywhere close to the real things we accomplish, because we have to evaluate goals and change them as our lives and priorities change. Really, many of the goals I had as a younger woman were flat-out wrong, not at all what God intended for my life. And many of the plans he had for me were far better than anything I could have dreamed up.

But let's take just a minute to write out a goal or two. Write them down here:

So why write your goals at all? Because this helps you find the *right* goals. Putting goals on paper helps you remember them, adjust

If you aim at nothing, you will surely hit it.

them as time goes on, and recognize your progress. As a result, your goals stay realistic and flexible, and they become an important part of planning for your future. Remember, if you aim at nothing, you will surely hit it.

Giving your goals "feet" is also important. One mistake I made early on in writing out my goals was that I wrote what I *wanted* out of life but neglected to write *how* to get there. The how-tos are key to actually making progress. They also may be the most difficult to write. Take some time to think and consider how you'll accomplish your goals, though, and you'll be surprised at what you can do. Trust me, it's worth the effort. A good plan with solid goals, stepping stones, and a realistic time table will eventually help you achieve the desires of your heart. Let's start right now with one simple goal for this year.

What is your top personal goal for this year? This may be a spiritual goal, like spending more time in prayer (that's mine). Or a relational goal, like spending less time with a toxic person (or more with one who inspires you). It may involve money, like the goal of one woman who wrote that she wanted to stop her "free-flowing finances." What is the issue or dream or desire niggling at your heart right now? Even if it seems bigger than you are, that's the one.

Now write one action step toward achieving it. Just one.

Example—Goal: Prayer; First Step: Schedule ten extra minutes each morning just for prayer.

1. My first *step* to achieve my goal is:

Keep your answer simple and attainable. Remember, we're taking baby steps right now (and this is just the first!), and as you accomplish this goal, then another, then another, you will find you are building the confidence to also rebuild your life, one goal at a time.

Strategy #5: Plan Each Day

Even with a good plan, success doesn't usually happen overnight. But it *will* happen—in smaller measures, each and every day—if you take time each day to plan and prioritize. List your top three things to do for the day, in order of priority.

In doing this, be sensitive to the leading of the Holy Spirit, who may have some different plans in mind. That means simply asking God, "What would you like me to do today?" and quieting your mind to listen. His plans may be quite different from yours.

After you've established the day's priorities, think about logistics. How can you accomplish these three things in the most efficient way? Instead of running from one side of town to the other and back again, map out your errands in advance. This will save you not only time but also gas! That's important in today's economy. Think about ways to accomplish two tasks in one location, if possible.

Planning is an area where technology really helps me out. If my plans are written in my PDA or computer, I'm much more likely to remember them. If my contacts can be found with a click of the mouse, I'm much more likely to call or email them. My husband is the opposite; he would no sooner carry a Palm or BlackBerry than ask for directions on a road trip. He does, however, make do with a written daily planner.

Whatever works for you: Outlook pop-ups telling you to go to a meeting, Excel worksheets neatly formatted, or a simple book where you can write your thoughts and activities for the day. Thoughtful planning will ultimately save you time and stress.

If you're not a plan type of girl, that's okay. We're beginning with the basics. In the space below write your top three things that must occur today (or if you're reading this later in the day, plan tomorrow), so that when you face the mirror at the end of the day, you'll feel good about what you accomplished. Is your laundry list of to-dos overwhelming you? Begin with one task for morning, one for the afternoon, and one for the evening. Think about the biggest, most important task—the thing your mind keeps returning to and your heart keeps nagging you about. Are they tasks that jive with your mission statement? Or tasks that free you up to pursue your mission statement? Stepping stones toward a goal? Cover those first. Jot down tomorrow's tasks now and see if you can follow through:

Morning:

Afternoon:

Evening:

Strategy #6: Schedule Unscheduled Time

I met a financial planner once who schedules his life into three differ-ent types of days: work days, buffer days, and free days. On work days he focuses on, well, work. On buffer days he does clean-up tasks such as organizing his office, finishing paperwork, writing thank-you notes, or making calls he hasn't had time for. Then free days are just that—free to do absolutely anything he wants. That's certainly one way to schedule, and he says it works brilliantly for him.

But here's another idea: how about allowing for a little bit of free time every day? Let's call it unscheduled time. Time to hang out with friends. Time to read a book or article. Time to write a note of en-couragement to a hurting friend. Just time. Listen once more to what one of our Balanced wrote: "Save enough time in each day/week, etc. so that there is no need to have to manage your time. There will always be free time in every day/week if you set aside time in each day that is not scheduled for anything."

The best hours for me to schedule free time are in the late after-noon. I do my best writing in the morning, and after about three o'clock I'm ready to chill out for a bit before I head into serious mommy time—dinner, homework, you know the drill. On the other hand, another writer I work with schedules her day exactly the oppo-site. She does her best writing at night when everyone is asleep and she can finally "hear the voice of God" in those quiet hours. Whatever strategy works best for you, make sure you're not so overscheduled that you can't take a few moments somewhere just to enjoy yourself. Relax and focus on something enjoyable. Try not to worry or think about what you'll do next or about other things you could be doing.

Strategy #7: Delegate, Delegate, Delegate

This is for you, Superwoman! It's time to step back and consider what it is that only you can do. Be realistic. If your kids are young, you might get away with claiming that if they wash the dishes, you'll just have to rewash them. Perhaps your husband doesn't make the bed according to your standards. Those are trivial things. But there have to be things that others can help with. Give your family credit for being at least somewhat intelligent and capable human beings! They really can make their own beds, stack their own dishes in the dishwasher, and put away their own clothes. Really.

To give yourself permission to receive help, look at the woman in Proverbs 31. She clearly had help. She knew how to delegate. No, we may never have "maidens" to help us around the house as she did. But is it possible to hire a housekeeper to help you out now and then? If the kids don't know how to make their own lunches, teach them! If your husband, a neighbor, or a fellow church member has offered to make you dinner, let them! If you have people working for you or administrative support personnel at your job, keep them busy! Reach out and get the help you need to make your life easier and better manage your time. If the woman in Proverbs 31 can delegate and accept help graciously, we can too.

Strategy #8: Unclutter Your Life

Procrastinators, this may also hit home for you. If you live in a home with tiny pieces of paper everywhere containing notes, numbers, or important information, you're probably frustrated by your disorganization. How many times do you spend hours trying to find a number you wrote down two days ago, or you realize a phone message you need to answer has disappeared? Worse yet, when you need to dispute a bill or find out about an overcharge, have you ever discovered that you've lost important information you'd written down? Talk about wasting time and creating a headache!

Clutter steals our time when we spend too much energy trying to find things that are in disarray. Not only do we waste time, but usually we end up stressed out and irritated too. I'm guilty! I'm still a recovering clutterholic.

You know the easiest way to deal with clutter? Just do it. Take five to ten minutes at the end of the day cleaning up your mess, just the way we would clean up the dishes after a meal. Have you ever heard of the Fly Lady? She almost has me convinced that decluttering can be fun. Almost. She suggests doing a "5 Minute Room Rescue" where we spend five minutes a day for the next twenty-seven days clearing a path in our worst room to create a place we are proud of.[3] Okay, that will work. Or, like my financial-planner friend, set aside a buffer day to handle the mess. Either way, this time spent cleaning up, filing, and organizing will absolutely save you more time later.

I know how hard the change can be, but it's time for us to throw away the junk, confront the little piles that seem to materialize around our house on their own, and get organized! Speaking of which, I'll get to that little pile sitting in my tray on my desk right after this chapter.

Strategy #9: Really Rest

We rush around five days a week, taking care of home and work responsibilities, and then the weekend comes. Ah . . . the weekend. Finally, we get our break. But Saturday morning begins with a soccer match for the youngest child while the oldest reminds you of a birthday party across town. Oops! That completely slipped your mind. Right after the soccer game you speed to Walmart to pick up a gift. While you're there, you grab a dessert for the church potluck dinner that night, hoping no one will notice you didn't bake it yourself.

Sunday morning arrives, and you're feeling frazzled and guilty. Aren't we supposed to feel spiritual on this day of rest? The church sermon gives you a few moments to relax—that is, when you're not jotting down your grocery list in the "sermon notes" section of the bulletin. You'll get to the day's shopping right after cleaning the bathrooms and starting at least one load of laundry.

Then Monday arrives . . . and you can't figure out why you're so tired after the weekend's "rest."

We've all heard about "keeping the Sabbath" or taking a day of rest and dedicating it to the Lord. This is actually one of the Ten Commandments. But it's also God's prescription for our own sanity. As Jesus pointed out, "The Sabbath was made for man, and not man for the Sabbath" (Mark 2:27 NASB).

However, observing a Sabbath doesn't mean you can't lift a finger or that you have to lounge around in bed all day. Jesus healed people on the Sabbath, although the religious leaders back then considered even this type of "work" to be taboo.

Jesus took the legalism out of this day of rest, but God's intention for the Sabbath has never changed. It should be a day of really resting and refocusing on the Lord and his purpose for your life. Time invested that really matters. Does it have to be a *Sunday*? No, I don't think so. Does it have to be an *entire* day? That's a question you'll have to answer for yourself. You'll also have to decide what "resting" truly means to you.

One of my younger friends, Terri, loves chillin' out by listening to soulful worship music. She has introduced me to some modern artists (like Jason Upton) who also bring refreshment to my spirit.

For me, real rest is also a time to read and pray. To give my work back to the Lord, surrendering it again to him. I'll be honest . . . there are still many weeks when I skip the Sabbath to take care of life's responsibilities. Bad move on my part, as I'm learning. When I do take this day of rest and surrender to the Lord my most valuable asset— my time—he always multiplies my productivity and clarity in the week to follow. I feel more rested and less stressed throughout the week. I think better, so I'm more efficient, saving more than the time I took to rest! Is there one day this week when you can just chill? Which day is it? Write it on your calendar now and get ready to be refreshed, maybe for the first time in years.

Strategy #10: Reflect

One of the reasons I feel less stressed after taking a Sabbath rest is because during my time of rest, I reflect on the previous week and what the Lord has taught me. I keep a journal and make notes about what I did well and where I tanked—my hits and misses. I think of ways I can improve, and I look for time stealers—people or projects that siphoned away minutes or hours that I didn't really recognize at the time.

It's during this time of reflection that I also review goals. Is my heart still in them? If not, I know I need to change them or change my attitude and actions. After prioritizing and monitoring my stepping-stone progress toward goals, I take a look ahead at the opportunity to design a new week. Consider your own past week and the one ahead. Then complete the statements below:

1. Last week, with the Lord's help, I aced this . . . (Come on, there has to be one thing you did well!)

2. "To err is human." This is how I tanked last week and what I learned from it:

3. Looking ahead to next week, I want to . . .

Reflection also brings gratitude. When I review the previous week, I gain new insight into how the Lord protected and provided for me, even when I felt the most alone. I see how he was in the details of my life. Reflection strengthens my faith because I take time to notice what God has done. In the rush of daily life, it's so easy to veer to the left or to the right of God's perfect plan. Pausing to reflect saves time by steering us back on track.

Ten More Tiny Time-Saving Tips

Ten + Ten = Time

10 More Tiny Time-Saving Tips

1. **Keep a notepad by the phone.**

2. **Ask questions now.**

3. **Delete useless emails.**

4. **Use your phone's memory dialing.**

5. **Books on tape.**

6. **Library books.**

7. **Call first.**

8. **Don't rush.**

9. **Automatic bill pay/online banking.**

10. **Online grocery shopping.**

We just reviewed the big-ten life changes that will help you take back time. Life Changing Seminars offered a radio program called *Redeeming the Time*.[4] These are some of the small, simple, and frankly quite brilliant ways they suggested to help us reduce the amount of time we waste.

1. *Notepad by the phone:* One thing we can do to communicate better is always have a notepad beside the phone. We often end up scrounging for an envelope or some other floating slip of paper to jot down important information. These randomly scrawled notes get misplaced or thrown away.

2. *Ask questions:* I'm all about asking the dumb questions, especially if you don't understand something someone is telling you. Ask for more specifics. Trying to do a project someone has asked you to do is a time waster if you don't know what you should be doing. Your assumptions might be on the wrong track, and a few simple clarifying questions can save you days. This tip also applies to asking for directions or details at the time of an invitation or making an appointment. Why call back later when you can get all your ducks in a row now?

3. *Delete useless emails:* A good friend of mine hates the computer! I try my best to help her through some basic technical concerns and questions, but one thing she hasn't overcome is the need to read every email regardless of how useless it is—even obvious spam. Don't even bother with those. Delete, delete, delete. (Or sign up for

a service such as Google's Gmail that is an excellent spam filter.) You're not missing anything, I promise!

4. *Use your phone's memory dialing:* Some numbers just aren't that easy to memorize. So program them into your phone instead of fumbling around every time you need to make that call. Make technology work for you!

5. *Books on tape:* As much as I love reading books, audio books are still a good idea for road trips or days spent running errands. Try it instead of constantly trying to find a radio station that's blaring obnoxious commercials.

6. *Library books:* Your local library should have a website where you can actually look up books to see if they're available or checked out. It also provides the location (library branch) of the book. Now that's not even the cool part. You can also reserve the book online! Then all you have to do at the library is go up to the counter and check out your books. And it's free! No more driving all the way there only to discover the book is checked out or at another branch all the way across town. Contact your local library to find out how you can enroll in their virtual library.

7. *Call first:* Just the other day I went to the store assuming it had what I was looking for. It didn't. As I wandered around for what felt like an eternity, I realized I should

have called first to see if the store had it in stock. A simple call can come in handy when you're looking for a special item.

8. *Don't rush:* I sometimes catch myself rushing or doing things quickly, believing this will save me time. Well, it doesn't. If anything, it robs me of time. When I rush around trying to do things, I usually end up breaking or forgetting something.

9. *Automatic bill pay/online banking:* I know a person who refuses to even mail checks. She spends an entire day running to the bank, to the electric company, and to the water department to drop off her payments on monthly bills. This to me is an obvious and frivolous waste of time. If your bank offers online banking, use it! You can *pay your bills in one click,* if your bills are the same each month. Even if they're not, it's as easy as clicking in the field and changing the amount or date. Also, most companies offer automatic bill pay to be taken directly from your account each month. You save time and money on check orders, envelopes, and stamps too!

10. *Online grocery shopping:* Yes, it's true. In major cities, you can now order your groceries online and have them delivered. I, for one, hate grocery shopping, and thankfully my husband handles this. If not, I would be the first person to sign up for this time-saving service. Search the web for an online grocer to see if this luxury is available in your town.

Those are some time-saving ideas to get you started, both the big stuff, like meeting with God, and the little stuff like online bill pay. Life is messy, but sometimes we make it messier—more complicated and stressful—than necessary. When we have multiple time wasters in our lives, we'll definitely feel overwhelmed, burned out, and unappreciated.

Our time is beyond valuable. Time is really all we have. How we fill it is our choice and our responsibility.

ACTION APPLICATION

For this week's Action Application, pick just one of the above smaller time-saving tips. Choose a time to get started on it and just do it! See if it doesn't add minutes or even hours to your life.

The Procrastinators

10 Smart Strategies to Overcome Time-Stealing Habits

I really want to do what is right, but I don't do it. Instead, I do the very thing I hate . . . But I can't help myself, because it is sin inside me that makes me do these evil things.

—ROMANS 7:15–17 THE BOOK

Ten + Ten = Time

Strategies to Overcome Time-Stealing Habits

Strategy #1: Don't Try This Alone.

Strategy #2: Recognize Your Responsibility.

Strategy #3: Realize the Battle Is in Your Mind.

Strategy #4 : Take Baby Steps.

Strategy #5: Determine Why You Started the Habit.

Strategy #6: Determine What the Habit Is Costing You.

Strategy #7: See It as a Choice Instead of a Habit.

Strategy #8: Find Something Else to Fill the Need.

Strategy #9: Stay the Course.

Strategy #10: Finish the Race

A NOTE FROM GOD

> *My Dear Procrastinating Daughter:*
>
> *I know you feel that you've simply lost your motivation—a victim of bad habits beyond your control. I know you are tired and can't remember the days when you had abundant energy. But I see the real problem—a root of fear and discouragement that has been planted in your heart. But my roots run deeper and stronger. I remember when you began listening to the world and its dispiriting messages instead of listening to the hopes and plans I have for your life. Come back to me, and I will help you find abundant life again. Or, maybe, for the first time. My perfect love will cast out any fear or discouragement you struggle with now or will ever face.*
>
> *Love always,*
> *God*

(From John 10:10, 1 John 4:18, Psalm 51:6)

Now with some basic time traps out of the way, let's go one step further. Instead of just looking at everyday time traps in the hustle and bustle of life, we'll explore the idea that our lives are an investment of time. What is it that's stealing years from your life? Stealing joy? Are you doing what you really want to do? In writing about doing the very things he hates, the apostle Paul is talking about sin in his life. We'll look at Paul's solution to this in a moment. First let's relate these words to ourselves when we invest our time in stuff that just doesn't matter. Stuff we don't want to do and at the end of the day leaves us saying "What happened?!"

Let's meet the Procrastinator. Her day goes a little something like this:

She wakes up and makes a mental list of the things she needs to do. She's thinking, *Today's the day I'm going to get a lot accomplished.*

As she gets dressed, she flips on the morning news and gets side-tracked by a story on the newest dieting trend. The story mentions a website she can visit for more information. Cool. She plops down at the computer to check it out. Looking at the clock, she knows she should be heading out the door, but she tells herself that she got up extra early anyway, so she actually has more time than she thinks.

As she inspects this new diet website, she spots an ad for a free laptop. And all she has to do is take the online quiz! Click, click, click . . . and thirty minutes later, she realizes she has to purchase three items that she doesn't want in order to get the laptop. *Humph, so much for "free."* Now, with two hours down the drain (and no laptop to show for it), she readjusts her schedule. She can go shopping tomorrow, right? In fact, that call to the cell-phone company about her overcharges can wait too. What's one more day?

She takes a shower, puts on her makeup, does her hair, and figures she'll just take a quick peek at her email before she heads off to her dental appointment. After reading some forwarded jokes and passing on a few of them to her friends, she types out a quick reply to a girlfriend in California. One has to keep in touch, after all.

Another glance at the clock: she's late for her appointment. She calls and reschedules it for next week. There's not much going on next week anyway, and this week is just so busy.

Free from the dental appointment, she's got some extra time! How about a few reruns of Seinfeld? It's just about to come on. An hour later, she's still watching TV and munching on potato chips, having been lured into a talk show involving a paternity dispute. She has lunch, then decides it's too hot to walk the dogs. She promises herself she'll get up earlier tomorrow to walk them.

Before the Procrastinator knows it, the sun has set and the day is gone. She hasn't accomplished a single thing on her mental to-do list but tells herself as she goes to sleep that she'll do it tomorrow. But tomorrow ends up following the same pattern as today did. Eventually she finds herself rushing around at the last minute, trying to get everything done at once.

Have you ever spent a day (or more) in the Procrastinator's shoes? And what's really going on below the surface?

Interestingly, these ladies in our survey don't feel overly stressed by external demands on their time, and they believe they have good systems and goals in place to manage themselves. What distinguishes this group is a habit of procrastinating. Simply put, these women know what to do—they understand how to set goals and take steps toward them—and feel comfortable managing time. *Many said they simply don't want to do it.* The women in this group tend to be a little older, most are over thirty-five, and many don't have children. Could it be they've lost sight of investing time where it really matters to them?

Today we often excuse our own destructive behaviors by saying, "Oh, it's just a bad habit. I simply can't control myself!" But let's examine this lame excuse for our actions, or lack thereof, and our wasted investment of time. Dr. Linda Mintle, a preeminent therapist, author, and my friend on the TV program *Living the Life,* told me that procrastination "can be rooted in your family, a response to an authoritarian figure such as a controlling father."[1] She says that procrastinators haven't learned to self-regulate, and putting things off or choosing not to solve their problems might be a form of rebellion. I'll let the doctor deal with the serious problems that require therapy and a comfy couch, and I'll focus instead on just one thing in this chapter: our habits. These can be disempowering actions that can rob us of investing our time wisely. It may begin with a single action, but it always ends in behavior that controls us.

Time and Chocolate

Disempowering Actions. Hmmm. Here's one of mine: I'm an emotional eater. Those who know me also know that I absolutely love chocolate! Blame it on hormones, blame it on stress, but nearly every day I feel drawn toward something or anything chocolate. Chocolate-chip cookies are my favorite, and I can't help it. It's part of who I am. Right? Wrong. It's merely a habit I've developed over the years. It is *not* who I am. The distasteful truth of the matter is that every time someone acquiesces and does something she would be better off not doing, she's making a choice.

Why is emotional eating a time factor, you ask? Because every extra cookie I stuff in my mouth means more time in the gym later. For years I carried an extra twenty-five pounds of baby fat (I used that excuse until my kids were in school) that robbed me of energy and quality of life. My back began to ache, and I suddenly didn't feel like playing with the kids as much. It also robbed me of time and motivation in solving my real problems. I felt badly, so I ate. Problem solved . . . for the moment. Have you ever thought of this kind of destructive behavior as procrastination? It was for me. It took me years to actually reverse this carb-craving, calorie-consuming trend that began with a simple habit of seeking food instead of seeking God— and I know it's something I'll probably always have to manage. Once we acknowledge that the things we do are changeable, we're one step closer to ending our bad habits. Unfortunately, it's only one small step of many that are needed to alter the things we find ourselves doing habitually.

Once we acknowledge that the things we do are changeable, we're one step closer to ending our bad habits.

If only it were as simple as recognizing the choice is ours, no one would ever have any bad habits. Instead, following recognition of that choice, we must exercise it—and that's where we trip and fall back into our comfortable routines.

So what's going on with these time-stealing, life-stealing habits we feel we can't control?

In a Rut, Literally

Surprisingly, there's a scientific reason behind the difficulty of changing our habits. Scientists at the Massachusetts Institute of Technology (MIT) have identified a neurological shift behind our resistance to breaking bad habits.[2] It's true. Basically, when you say you're in a rut, you're more right than you may have realized. Think of the wheel tracks you can still spot in some areas of prairie where the wagon trains came through—more than a hundred years ago! Essentially, doing the same thing over and over (like one wagon after another) creates a neurological pathway that becomes more and more ingrained in our bodies and minds. This pathway makes it easier and easier to slide into that groove of behavior—it becomes the path of least resistance (like one wagon breaking ground for another). Voila! Habits are formed.

According to the scientists conducting this study, habits and addictions form these pathways in the basal ganglia, the same part of the brain that helps us learn by repetition. In the study, done on rats, the basal ganglia sparked to life while the rodents were first learning how to travel through a maze. But as time wore on and the rats learned the way, the basal ganglia quieted down. The rats had formed pathways in their brains to guide them so they could get through the maze with limited intellectual input.

It's a bit like driving home from work for the thousandth time. How many times have you put the car into drive, pointed it in the right direction, and before you knew it, you were in your driveway trying to remember how you got there? Scary to think about, really, but the truth is that the brain doesn't want to work any more than the rest of your body does. People slouch because it's easier than standing up straight, and they stand with their lower back swayed because it relaxes the rest of the back, making it easier on the muscles. Even the most active among us is built for conservation of energy, and the brain does the same thing.

This is not all bad. Sometimes this routine pathway in your brain works to your favor—like being able to get ready in the morning with minimal thought before the first cup of coffee. God designed us this way to allow us to train our bodies and minds to do good things over and over again with less and less energy—like when we prepare for an athletic competition or develop better conversation or oratory skills or learn how to take care of children. But at other times this tendency or habit can be a major detriment to your life.

10 Time-Stealing Habits to Think About:

1. Do I have any health habits (like Carolyn's emotional eating) that are stealing my quality of life now and potentially for years in the future?

2. Do I have a habit of spending way too much time watching sitcoms at night?

3. Do I have a habit of spending way too much time on the computer?

4. Do I have a habit of answering email throughout the day, whenever anyone wants my time?

5. Do I have a habit of putting off important family or work projects until the very last minute?

6. Do I have a habit of running late every morning and then blaming it on "crazy traffic"?

7. Do I have a habit of letting little clutter piles turn into giant, intimidating clutter piles?

8. Do I have a habit of answering every phone call right away instead of accepting that voice mail is my friend?

9. Do I have a habit of letting toxic people steal way too much of my time?

10. Do I have a habit of putting off spending time with the people I really want to be with?

"The key to breaking a bad habit and adopting a good one is making changes in our daily life that will minimize the influence of the now and remind us of the later," writes Mary Ann Chapman in *Psychology Today*. But making a shift like that in our thinking is pretty tough and can often feel impossible or overwhelming.

We're not the only ones who struggle to make changes. Chapman describes a study conducted by Howard Rachlin, PhD, of the State University of New York at Stony Brook: "Working in a laboratory with pigeons . . . [he] found that when birds were given a simple choice between immediate and delayed reward, they chose the immediate reward 95 percent of the time. This was true even though the delayed reward (food) was twice the size of the immediate one."[3] Gives a whole new meaning to being birdbrained! But here's the great news: you are not an animal. You were created in the image of God. The fact remains that we have power to master our choices and take charge of our lives, and that's something to be reckoned with. The question now is how to break free of those deep ruts in our brains and make some positive changes in how we live.

You may not like the sound of this, but the best, most effective way to shed unwanted habits doesn't involve a single action or miracle cure, but rather a process. Just like it took time to dig that groove in the brain, it takes time—and effort—to scoot off in another direction. The good news is that the progression of steps is fairly simple. I've boiled it down to a ten-step plan for your success.

Strategy #1: Don't Try This Alone

Back to the apostle Paul and his tell-it-like-it-is letter to the Romans:

> I know I am rotten through and through so far as my old sinful nature is concerned. No matter which way I turn, I can't make myself do right. I want to, but I can't. When I want to do good, I don't. And when I try not to do wrong, I do it anyway. But if I am doing what I don't want to do, I am not really the one doing it; the sin within me is doing it. It seems to be a fact of life that when I want to do what is right, I inevitably do what is wrong. I love God's law with all my heart. But there is another law at work within me that is at war with my mind. This law wins the fight and makes me a slave to the sin that is still within me. Oh, what a miserable person I am! Who will free me from this life that is dominated by sin? Thank God! The answer is Jesus Christ our Lord. (Romans 7:18–25 THE BOOK)

According to Paul, as humans we naturally rebel and do the very things we hate. But through the sacrifice of Jesus Christ, we're freed from this cycle and restored to the position of power over our own choices. It begins with a choice to accept that truth. In Christ, we're brand-new creations, and we no longer have to be controlled by our sinful nature. Instead, we can be guided by the Spirit of God living within us.

Here's a profound prayer to get you started: *Help!*

Seriously. God will help you when you ask him and humble

yourself enough to admit that you can't control yourself on your own. I have another friend who is a writer and was procrastinating on finishing her project, even though her deadline was just a month away. All of it seemed too big to handle, and she said she just couldn't get motivated to work on it. The more we talked, the more we both realized that she was facing discouragement. The fear of failure. The feeling of "I can't do this on my own and why in the world would the Lord care about my little book anyway?" This is a woman who is used to solving the problems of other people, and in finally admitting her own fears, slowly her discouragement began to lift. The key was realizing that this wasn't just another project; this was an assignment from her benevolent Friend and Creator who would also help her accomplish it. One step at a time.

You might be reading this and also wondering, *Why would the Creator of the universe actually spend time helping me break a tiny bad habit?* Because he cares for you—and he cares about the small stuff too. Just in case you think I'm making that up, check out 1 Peter 5:7: "Cast all your anxiety on him because he cares for you" (NIV). He even cares about those of us who procrastinate, putting off the important areas of life (like learning to be healthy again) because they seem just too big to handle. Remember, in Christ we're no longer slaves to our rebellious nature. We don't have to succumb to discouragement or fear. We are powerful beyond comprehension, even powerful enough to overcome our destructive little habits that threaten to derail us.

Even if you don't believe that right now, remember my friend who decided to take just one more step. Harriet Beecher Stowe once said, "When you get into a tight place and everything goes against you, till it seems as though you could not hang on a minute longer, never give up then, for that is just the place and time that the tide will turn."[4]

Write just one habit you would love to kick that steals your time and motivation. Just one. The one you can't seem to control. It may be directly related to your everyday schedule, like constantly being late for meetings. It may be related to the quality of your time and health, like my emotional-eating problem. Begin your journey to overcome this action by praying this simple prayer: *Lord, _____ is one area that I hate about my life. I can't seem to control it. But you promise that we are more than conquerors through your Son. I know that you love me, and today I surrender this disempowering habit to you. Thank you that today we begin our first step toward victory in the name of Jesus. Amen.*

Strategy #2: Recognize Your Responsibility

I wasn't able to manage my unhealthy eating habit until I got down on my knees and asked for God's help. Again, I'm not saying that I've totally kicked it. Overcoming my habit is a work in progress requiring daily management. God will provide the power we need, but it's up to us to take daily action. In other words, we have to accept responsibility.

The only way you'll ever change things in your life is to accept responsibility for your part in the problem. My habit of emotional eating began by wanting immediate relief to life's pressures. Your problem with procrastination may stem from having too much on your plate as a stressed-out young student or single mom, so you choose to do nothing at all. Understandable. And many times, habits can begin as a result of situations that are beyond our control, someone else's choices, or maybe even genetic predispositions. (Chocolate! Okay, I'm stretching here.) But continuing to engage in these habits every day of your life, well past the historical jump-start—well, that's all *us,* I'm afraid. Many women in our survey grasped that, listing their part in time traps:

"Laziness and slow metabolism."
"Just not having the energy."
"Not motivated enough."
"Lack of interest."
"Poor management."

For other women in our survey, it was disorganization or a feeling of being overwhelmed that kept them in a time-wasting, procrastinating mode.

Now we have a choice: own up to our portion of the blame and seek God's help to overcome our habits, or remain in slavery to them for the rest of our lives. Here are a couple of questions to ask yourself: *How have I contributed to getting stuck in the one habit I named above? What one step can I take today to change this?*

Strategy #3: Realize the Battle Is in Your Mind

Together with God, you *can* change your habits! Do you really believe that?

Not only are we responsible for our actions, we're responsible for

Focus on the potential for success, take responsibility in the process, and you'll kick your bad habits.

our thoughts, which will also be key for the Self-Stressed women. The secret to successful time management is to adjust your mental attitude to one of *possibility*. You have to *think* you're going to do it in order for you to do so. Focus on the potential for success, take responsibility in the process, and you'll kick your bad habits.

Once you've reset your brain into the positive mode of thinking, you'll find you have more control over how well you handle urges and habits that before seemed insurmountable. Jumping out of those ridiculous ruts we've put ourselves in will begin to seem ridiculously simple.

When it comes to the business world, I've interviewed executives who believe there really aren't any good habits—since a habit by definition is something done without thinking about it, and who wants to be known as someone who doesn't pay attention? I can see their point. What we often call "good work habits" are actually constant, conscious efforts to do things in a way that benefits everyone, and they should be recognized as something more than a rote response to stimuli. People who pay their bills on time every month and pay attention to meeting deadlines are people who think about what they're doing before they take action. They have control over their lives in a way that propels them forward in a positive direction.

To put bad habits to rest, we have to deliberately think about our actions and make a conscious effort each day—or maybe each hour or every few minutes—to choose the *right* path instead of the *habitual* path.

One of the greatest champions of positive change and action was the groundbreaking minister Norman Vincent Peale. An author of dozens of life-affirming books and booklets as well as the creator of *Guideposts* magazine, his most important legacy is the belief in personal strength through thinking positive thoughts. Having walked the walk (he experienced horribly poor self-esteem as a child), Peale set out to help others find the path toward a better life. He believed that there was nothing that couldn't be done if you had the right attitude. "Throw back the shoulders, let the heart sing, let the eyes flash, let the mind be lifted up, look upward and say to yourself . . . Nothing is impossible!" He had an amazing way of seeing life that showed millions the way to success. His motto: "Become a possibilitarian. No matter how dark things seem to be or actually are, raise your sights and see possibilities—always see them, for they're always there."[5]

> *"Become a possibilitarian. No matter how dark things seem to be or actually are, raise your sights and see possibilities—always see them, for they're always there."*
>
> *—Normal Vincent Peale*

My mom is also a possibilitarian. When I was young, she always used to tell me that I could do anything I set my mind to. I guess I was silly enough to believe her. She and Mr. Peale had something in common. They recognized that life was not all good. Sometimes life really stinks, but we choose our attitudes through the challenges. So rather than bemoaning all the reasons why things won't work, become a "possibilitarian" and focus on how to make them work. There's always a way; it's just a matter of finding the road to get you there. And remember, the battle really is in your mind, and it's a battle you can win.

Strategy #4: Take Baby Steps

The Little Engine That Could wasn't just a story, you know. Just as the little engine took on the huge mountain one railroad tie at a time, we need to learn to see our challenges in bite-size pieces in order to overcome them. (I told you I think about food most of the time.)

Seriously. We tend to build up our problems into huge monstrosities that have no real beginning, middle, or end. It's so easy to feel overwhelmed by a situation or problem when you look at the entire thing in one big block. But once you break down the idea of changing your habits into manageable portions—baby steps—the possibility of moving beyond who you are now and becoming who you want to be gets much clearer. Each portion, then, doesn't look as intimidating. By starting with small steps, you can focus on taking control over each little part. Then one day . . . you realize you've conquered all the parts!

For example, all of us emotional eaters can first get rid of the comfort food in the house. That's baby-step one. Buy some healthy alternatives. Baby-step two. Find an alternate way to deal with stress, like taking a walk, a much better investment of time anyway. Baby-step three.

See, you *can* do this! It may not go exactly as you think it should, and you might make a few mistakes, but the point is that whatever bad habits you have *can* be overcome if you break down your strategy into manageable steps.

This method is different than the usual "If you *really* want to quit, you will." Instead of focusing on what you can stop—the end result—hone in on your own choices and how they affect what you want to have happen. In other words, what are the baby steps you are taking to result in this overall action? When you do that, and you recognize your own control in the matter, it becomes easier to stop the behavior.

This process of taking one baby step at a time helps us maintain courage and stamina for the long trip up the "mountains" of bad habits in our lives.

Strategy #5: Determine Why You Started the Habit

Most of us didn't just decide one day to develop a lazy mental process or destructive behavior; our habits started for a reason . . . usually wanting something positive or fearing something negative. Initially we filled a need by doing these things. In other words, bad habits stem from a positive feedback loop. You get something positive from doing what you're doing, which isn't a bad thing in itself. The problem is that the pleasure from your bad habits is short-term, and once you look at the bigger long-term picture, you'll find that these habits hurt you more than they make you feel good.

Did I mention that I enjoy the occasional double-chocolate fudge ice cream sundae with nuts and three cherries on top? But if I indulge in one too often—say, daily (remember my love of chocolate!)—I know I'm going to gain a ton of weight. I'll have less energy for the things I love. On top of that, I'm going to hate looking in the mirror and my next investment of time will be spent learning about the newest diet on the market. Again.

The solution to ending our bad habits lies in discovering what we find so enticing about the actions in the first place. What need does a delicious dessert fill in my life? What is it I'm trying to obtain . . . or hide from? How about you?

As I said, most habits come from one of two places: a desire for a positive response or a fear of a negative one. Either desire or fear can create a positive or a negative reaction in your life. Brian Tracy, author of sixteen books on achieving personal success, believes that the habits formed by a desire for positive things in your life most often lead to life-enhancing decisions. Habits that stem from your fears do just the opposite, he says. "They hold you back. They interfere with your success. They trip you up on a regular basis. They cause you to sell yourself short and settle for far less than your potential."[6]

Beware especially the habits that can easily slide into addiction. We know that toying with them might result in a dangerous behavior with very bad long-term consequences. Social drinking might become full-blown alcoholism. Cigar smoking (even among women these days!) can become an addiction to cigarettes. Viewing R-rated movies might desensitize us to soft porn. Online gambling might become secret gambling in the casino down the road.

God calls us to do the things he asks. If we're absorbed in bad habits, or even addictions, where will we find the time and energy to go after his goals for us? And then, where does our life investment go? Into places we'd rather not think about—often relationship disintegration, job loss, financial loss, spiritual depravity. Is this how you want your life to be defined? No, me either.

So what is driving *your* habit? Short-term positive feelings? Fear of letting yourself or others down? (Many of our women who procrastinate say they spend "too much time on the computer" as a way to hide from life's challenges.) Finding the answer will be the key to ending this life-stealing habit.

So how do you figure out what fears you're dodging (or what positive responses you're seeking) by engaging in your habits? By paying very close attention to your emotions and your state of mind when you fall into that habitual behavior. What (or who) goes through your mind when you think about your habit? How do you feel, both physically and mentally, when you're doing these things? What's your immediate reaction to the idea of stopping this habit? Does it make you feel nervous? Do you already have a list of excuses or objections? What do you feel you would lose if you stopped right now? There's a reason you continually feed this neurological path, and somewhere deep in the recesses of those very ruts is where you'll find it.

It may be a surprise to you to discover that just in the process of analyzing our true motivations we can almost immediately begin to alter our behavior.

Dr. David Gershaw, author of *Breaking Bad Habits,* suggests that after you've done this soul-searching, you should do what you can to remove whatever is reinforcing the bad habit. "You need to remove, avoid or delay the reinforcement," he says.[7] This will alleviate the need to do the negative behavior, as the short-term positives will no longer be present. (I guess that means Twinkies can no longer live in my pantry.)

It's up to us to face our own weaknesses and take positive action to overcome them. This is where you start to make a plan, laying out your responsibility and the baby steps you can take.

1. Why did I start this habit anyway?

2. What is my positive feedback from it, or what am I trying to avoid?

3. How can I replace this habit with a better investment of time?

Begin thinking about these questions, and in this chapter's Action Application we'll get down to details about this habit. Sometimes just realizing why we are doing what we're doing brings healing and change.

Strategy #6: Determine What the Habit Is Costing You

It's all well and good to analyze our habits and realize we need to change. But the connection between thinking and doing is *motivation*. Many women wrote us that this is their biggest problem. Usually we're not motivated to act unless we see that it's in our best interests, that we have something to gain. When it comes to overcoming bad habits, what we stand to gain is no longer having to pay the price or experience the negative consequences of these detrimental behaviors.

So what is your habit costing you? Just as in doing a budget for your finances, you get a true perspective on what your habit is costing you. Let's break down the costs that result from your habit.

For smokers, it's fairly simple to work this out. I had a friend, a coworker, with a nicotine habit. The habit became a severe addiction, so severe he was smoking on his deathbed. For him, the lifetime cost was about forty years. For your pocketbook, at around $4.60 per pack of cigarettes, if you smoke one pack every day, that's roughly $1,700 every year. Some smokers go through two packs a day or more! My friend paid more for life and health insurance too. Add up the dollars wasted, and that alone is a pretty good reason to quit.

In terms of lifetime negative investment, smoking changed my friend's senses, his ability to smell and taste. He reeked of tobacco, and smoke often surrounded him in a cloudy haze, so his habit quite possibly kept him from developing life-investment-worthy relationships. (Nonsmoking is a top factor for most people when they seek a mate.) Add to that the necessary breaks in his work day, which made him less efficient, and he was losing on yet another front. Did he miss a promotion? A raise? Who knows.

When you look at all those costs compared with the relatively small and temporary perceived benefits to smoking, it really boggles the mind, doesn't it? And believe me, *every habit has similar time and quality-of-life costs.*

Unfortunately, most people with bad habits don't examine the costs. They just continue in them without thinking. Oh, they may think about the financial cost every now and then, when the checkbook is low. Or they may recognize the social stigmas occasionally. But by themselves, those reasons aren't often enough to motivate for a change of habit. You really have to look at the big picture and see every aspect of your life that's affected by your habit to truly be motivated to change.

10 Costs of a Habit

Look at the problem through various lenses. Consider each of the following perspectives, and how each area of life is affected by your bad habits:

1. *Spiritual*—Is this habit honoring to God and his workmanship (i.e., your body)? Are you depending on this habit to comfort you or alleviate stress instead of trusting God to help you?

2. *Time*—How many months or years would you save/ be able to put into something more productive if you did not engage in this habit?

3. *Energy*—How much time do you spend every day trying to cover up or overcome the problems of your bad habits?

4. *Your Daily Time*—How much of your time each day would you save or be able to put to something more productive if you did not engage in this habit?

5. *Self-esteem*—How do you feel about yourself when you do these things?

6. *Family*—In what ways do your habits affect your partner, children, parents, siblings, or friends?

7. *Health*—How do your habits affect your body? Consider how some habits may have a more subtle or indirect effect, such as increasing your stress level.

8. *Social*—Does this in any way limit your ability to make or keep friends?

9. *Financial*—Is this habit costing you money in terms of employment, career advancement, or outright funds to buy or replace items as needed?

10. *Mental well-being*—How much more joyful would you be if the bad habit weren't a part of your life? How would your opinion of yourself be affected if you were to overcome this habit?

Recognizing the true cost to your life can make the biggest impression on your need to break bad habits and create the motivation required to make the change.

Strategy #7: See It as a Choice Instead of a Habit

Once you've figured out how this habit started and laid out the pros and cons of it, you can no longer claim to have no control. Sorry, but at this stage of the game you're more than aware of what's going on. Unlike Ivan Pavlov's dog, you know that the bell may not necessarily mean food, so the automatic response shouldn't be the same. Instead, you get to start making choices.

Speaking of that munching pup, let's go back to my example of emotional eating. How often has it happened that you've sat down on the couch to watch your favorite movie only to remember that you've forgotten the most important part, POPCORN! The movie is paused in the DVD player while the microwave sizzles and pops. A glass of soda to wash down the salty, buttery goodness, and you're finally good to go. For some people, the idea of watching a movie without popcorn is like taking a bath without soap. It's just not something one does.

Aha! Not true! It's a habit we've formed for some reason, probably costing us extra pounds and cholesterol each year, not to mention quality relaxation time with a good movie (or chore time after it's done!). But now we've realized we have the power and tools to break out of this habit.

If you're like me, eating while watching a movie is a habitual response to an action. It's what we do because it's what we've always done. But when I began looking at all food entering my mouth as a choice I was making, everything changed. Think about it. What if you decide that you'll eat only when you can actually enjoy the food, paying close attention and enjoying every morsel? That choice will mean no more habitual eating, because when you eat by habit, you're doing it without conscious thought. Believe it or not, this will also make it easier to choose better foods, because you won't be eating to fill a void but rather to exclusively satiate your hunger. That means a healthier you and me. Is there a better investment of time than this?

The same concepts apply to other habits as well. A man I once interviewed overcame his couch-potato ways by watching TV while exercising on the treadmill. Would you believe he lost more than one hundred pounds in one year? Another friend is overcoming her shopping addiction by carrying only cash into her favorite stores. This one is a work in progress, but hey, she's making a step. I am overcoming my clutter procrastination habit by cleaning up my desk on Fridays. Okay, I'm not the Fly Lady, but give me a break, it's another step!

Pray for God's power over your habit and make a firm decision to take control. Make choices that have even better rewards than your habitual actions do. You'll be in a better position to fight your engrained tendencies and instead work at creating new paths that benefit you and those you love. It doesn't end there. These choices have to be made over and over again until the new choice takes the place of the old habit. This is the "action stage." It's letting go of the lazy way of doing things and starting to take charge of your actions. Here's where we take pride in the changes we're seeing and start recognizing the benefits of our new good habits. This is the time of triumph, and we get to rejoice in it! Other people will recognize the changes in you too. Making positive choices can improve your health (mental, emotional, physical, or spiritual), give you more time with family and friends, and shift how people see you.

As time moves on, the choices are easier and easier to make, but remember to stay vigilant. Although Normal Vincent Peale claimed that the mind quickly responds to teaching and discipline, some experts say that it takes twenty-one days of doing something to make it a habit, and thirty days to overcome a bad habit already in place. I suppose it's a matter of perspective, but I'm not sure I agree that twenty-one to thirty days is "quickly." Certainly not in our drive-thru world! Other researchers contend that it takes six months of constant vigilance to make those changes as engrained as the previous bad habits were.

But when you think it through a little more, it's really not so bad. Just think about how long you've been entrenched in your old habits. How much time have you wasted? How does that length of time compare to a mere thirty days? I probably spent a decade trapped in unhealthy eating habits.

So don't give up yet! And don't discount what you've accomplished just because the results aren't immediate either. The thing is, if you've made it to this stage of the game, you're already ahead of most.

Remember that bad habits come about because of the lure of short-term gain with no regard for the long-term effects. By making the decision to change those habits, you're making a decision to look beyond the here and now. The action part of creating good habits encompasses all parts of the mental process, from figuring out why you're doing it, to knowing what you're giving up and what you'll gain with that sacrifice, making the choice to do so, and consciously being happy about the changes in your life.

Sounds pretty tough—and it is, on some levels. But if it means a happier, healthier, more successful life, the end result is worth it, isn't it?

Strategy #8: Find Something Else to Fill the Need

While these positive decisions come with a cost, what if there's a way to lessen the fee?

We talked about the payoff that your bad habit was giving you. Now's the time to find something else to fill that need. Giving up the habit will leave a gaping hole in your daily life, and if you don't fill it with something, it will be incredibly difficult to stick to your new way of doing things. Whether it's procrastination or emotional eating or spending way too much time surfing the net, there's a reason you do it, and that reason has to be addressed with something that doesn't have the same negative effects as the bad habits you're trying desperately to shed.

For example, I replaced my need for chocolate by snacking on protein bars when the urge arises. Okay, true, some of them taste like sawdust, but others can almost pass for an authentic candy bar. Of course, the better choice would be to replace the chocolate with fruits or vegetables, but give me a break—it's a baby step! It has also helped me keep my weight down and has given me more energy for the kids. If your habit is spending every evening on the computer, how about finding a positive alternative? Go out and meet real, live people. Take a class. Volunteer at a shelter.

Most doctors agree that repeated substitution will break our routines in the same way that we developed the bad habits. It's that whole thing about creating a new pattern in our brain. Finding a new groove . . . literally.

Now let's go a little deeper into this groove. Consider kids and how they process frustration. It's all well and good to *tell* a child to stop throwing a temper tantrum, but if you don't *give* her a better way to get your attention, she'll go back to screaming, because it meets her immediate need. You may not like it, and she may get in trouble for it, but she does get your attention—which is what she wanted in the first place. If this behavior isn't corrected quickly, it can easily become a destructive habit. Really, this is the crux of almost all bad habits! We're trying to meet a need in a way that we know gets results, even if the results may not be exactly what we were looking for. So find another way to meet that need, a way that works more effectively and doesn't lead to negative feedback.

Rita Emmett has written a helpful book called *The Procrastinating Child*. She targets many reasons kids put things off, including fear of the unknown, fear of failure, fear of success, fear of being rejected, and the list goes on. She says once a fear is "recognized and has a name, the procrastination often disappears without our working on or struggling with it.[8] Fear is replaced with acceptance. Fear is exchanged for success, accomplished just one step at a time.

So let's learn from the children. What can I do to replace my need for attention? What can I do to replace my fear of failure, which leads me to do nothing? If you can't think of something to do instead of your habit, ask for ideas from some folks who care about you. This will spark your creativity and bring others alongside you to support the changes you're trying to make. Remember my friend who was having a problem completing her writing project because of fear and discouragement? She replaced her habit of procrastination by recognizing the possibility that her book would help others and that she could not only finish the book, but succeed.

Strategy #9: Stay the Course

Going back to our MIT scientists, you'll remember that their study identified how habits create trails in our brain, making it possible to do things without much thought. What may not have come across in all this talk about creating new pathways is the fact that the old pathways still exist—they haven't been erased just because we made a new road.

Oh fun, right? So although we've spent thirty days doing everything we can to get out of a habit, they're saying the negative thing didn't really go away completely? Maybe. My temptation to be an emotional eater will likely be something I have to consciously manage daily for the rest of my life, with God's help, much like an alcoholic is never "recovered" but rather "recovering." You may also be tempted to relapse into bad habits—into doing nothing because it feels much safer that way. Once you realize you have this tendency, that you are a recovering procrastinator, it will be much easier to tackle the problem. You've been here before and succeeded!

Ann Graybiel, the Walter A. Rosenblith professor of neuroscience in MIT's Department of Brain and Cognitive Sciences, describes this lingering temptation: "It is as though, somehow, the brain retains a memory of the habit context, and this pattern can be triggered if the right habit cues come back. This situation is familiar to anyone who is trying to lose weight or to control a well-ingrained habit. Just the sight of a piece of chocolate can reset all those good intentions."[9] Oh, how true!

This explains yo-yo dieting or quitting smoking or "falling off the wagon" for the umpteenth time, doesn't it? The new pathways are in place, but the older ones are so much more comfortable that the brain simply prefers them. It's like grabbing your favorite robe, old and tattered, to snuggle into on a bad day, leaving your beautiful new robe in a heap on the floor. You want warm fuzzies and comfort that come only from old routines. These are the kinds of things to be wary of during the rough times.

For decades your habits have been part of your hardwiring. But here's the difference and the triumph: *you know it now*. You're aware of it. Diligence, awareness, and prayer (not necessarily in that order) will keep those habits at bay. Keep going during this last lap. Focus on the positive changes going on, and don't give up. If something should happen to throw things out of whack again, don't let discouragement take root again! One nosedive off the wagon doesn't make a relapse . . . unless you allow it to.

Norman Vincent Peale recommends, "Start each day by affirming peaceful, contented and happy attitudes and your days will tend to be pleasant and successful." I would add that you should also reaffirm your dedication to the changes you've made. It might seem silly, but those little self-talks can go a long way toward maintaining a healthy mind-set.

Strategy #10: Finish the Race

However many bad habits you're able to identify, my experience is that success comes by dropping one at a time. Finish one race before beginning another.

It's that baby-step philosophy again. Focus on the most costly of your habits in terms of time, energy, money, success, and personal advancement. Once you and the Lord have stuffed that one into the ground, you'll be stronger and better prepared to deal with the next one, or even a couple of smaller habits at once, if you feel up to it. Regardless, you'll have proven what you're capable of, and none of your behaviors will ever seem that impossible to defeat again.

I am happy to tell you that my friend has finished her book and signed with another company to write several additional books. Talk about stuffing procrastination into the ground! Making changes in our lives is an ongoing process that should never end. The truth is that losing these negative traits is just one aspect of the maturing and growing process of life. We'll never be perfect until we get to heaven.

Even the apostle Paul cut himself some slack:

I'm not saying that I have this all together, that I have it made. But I am well on my way, reaching out for Christ, who has so wondrously reached out for me. Friends, don't get me wrong: By no means do I count myself an expert in all of this, but I've got my eye on the goal, where God is beckoning us onward—to Jesus. I'm off and running, and I'm not turning back. (Philippians 3:12–14 MSG)

So press on. Take responsibility for all your habits. It will be the beginning of a new journey of investing your time in choices and behaviors that empower your success.

ACTION APPLICATION
Testing Your Habits

What are some of your bad habits or things you do often that seem to be a bad use of your time?

Now pick one of the habits that you want to start changing. Which one seems the most costly? (You won't be successful if you try to defeat all of them at once.)

With the habit you've chosen, where, when, or why do you think you started doing this?

What aspect of this habit do you need to take personal responsibility for? (Depending on your answer, you may want to pray and ask for God's forgiveness about your part in creating this problem. You may also want to take time to forgive whoever else may have had a part in forming this habit in your life.)

What does this habit cost you? Remember to consider the following areas of your life: health, spiritual, mental well-being, self-esteem, family, social, career, financial, energy, and your time.

What are some baby steps you can take to start changing this habit? What small choices can you begin making to help you overcome this behavior?

What can you do or use to replace this habit? How could you fill this need in a positive, healthy way?

The Pressured

10 Smart Strategies for Stellar Decision Making

Discretion will protect you, and understanding will guard you.
—PROVERBS 2:11 NIV

Ten + Ten = Time

Strategies for Stellar Decision Making

Strategy #1: Simply Ask for Wisdom.

Strategy #2: Review Your Mission.

Strategy #3: Define the Real Problem.

Strategy #4: Dare to Risk.

Strategy #5: Consider Your Sources (Seek Wise Counsel).

Strategy #6: Consider Your Biases.

Strategy #7: Consider All Possible Solutions.

Strategy #8: Consider the Consequences.

Strategy #9: Listen to Your Gut (Maybe).

Strategy #10: Act on Your Decisions.

A NOTE FROM GOD

My Dear Pressured Daughter:

I understand. I was despised and forsaken by those I came to love and save. I was looked down upon and passed over. I was a man who suffered and knew pain firsthand. I carried their sorrows, but they thought I was being punished for my own sins and failings. I was beaten and tortured, but I didn't say a word.

I understand your confusion. Life is coming at you from a hundred different directions. If you just ask me, I'll help you make all these choices that seem too hard to handle on your own. You were never meant to go through this alone. Put your trust firmly in me, and we will overcome these pressures together, one at a time. I'm waiting for your time.

Love always,

Jesus

(From Isaiah 53 and Matthew 11:28–29)

Do you ever read advice columns? Take a look at this one from "Annie's Mailbox":

Dear Annie: I am 36 and have been dating "Steve" off and on for two years. Most of the "off" times were because he wanted to date other women. I finally moved on and began dating again, when lo and behold, Steve asked me to marry him. He said he was ready to commit because he didn't want to lose me to someone else. Since accepting his proposal, however, my joy has been clouded by this feeling that he's going to call things off as soon as he finds someone more attractive. We were both working hard toward rebuilding trust when I found out Steve is still in contact with the woman he left me for in April. They call each other and send joke e-mails. I confronted him, and after he initially denied it, he said that since his son is in the same class as hers, it is OK for him to be in touch about school, etc. Annie, I do not yet have children, but I think that each of them [Steve and his ex] could find other parents in class to talk to. He says asking him to sever ties with this woman is irrational. I am ready to call off the engagement, but I don't want to make what might be a huge mistake. Am I asking too much?—*Mixed Emotions in Mississippi*

Dear Mixed Emotions: Here's our frank assessment: Steve is not a good marriage risk. He's not trustworthy. He doesn't make you feel confident and secure. He doesn't put your feelings first. We predict you will be having serious marital difficulties within a few years. It's your choice what to do about it now.—*Annie*[1]

And here's how I would answer Mixed Emotions: "Save time and dump him now!" (I guess that's why I don't write advice columns about love!) It's so much easier to solve other people's problems, isn't it? It's much harder when the choice is ours.

As if life didn't already have enough obstacles and challenges involving our time, we're faced with an unending number of important decisions to make on how, where, and with whom to invest our days. Like "Mixed Emotions," we make decisions about our loved ones (whom we'll marry, how we'll raise a family, whom to spend time with as friends), our life's work (how we want to invest our time, where we want to work—in or out of the home), where we'll live, what kind of car we'll drive, and whether we'll shovel or use a snowblower (just checking to see if you were still with me!). We'll explore these top priorities in part three, minus the snowblower.

But right now, let's get really honest about our time choices. Sometimes none of our options are easy to swallow. Sometimes choices are made for us, like it or not. But in this chapter, my Pressured friends, it's all about the *decisions* you are responsible for, which can be daunting, like these ladies wrote:

> "I have many interests, hobbies, friends, family members, and responsibilities that all require a balancing of my time—it means lots of juggling and arranging."

> "Unscheduled interruptions or priorities. Exhaustion or lack of cooperation, usually from children or outside influences, e,g., traffic, grocery lines, etc."

> "Not being able to stay on task, something always pulls me away from what I'm trying to concentrate on at the moment."

Sure. A lot of this stuff we can't control, but in this chapter we'll focus on what we can.

Don't Throw Your Pearls (*of Time*) Before Swine

The italicized words are mine in the above headline, but believe it or not, the other words are straight from the mouth of Jesus, "Do not give what is holy to dogs, and do not throw your pearls before swine, or they will trample them under their feet, and turn and tear you to pieces" (Matthew 7:6 NASB).

I always thought this verse was extremely harsh. After all, aren't we supposed to help people? To be kind to everyone? Sure. But that isn't what Jesus is talking about here. Mainly, he's talking about discernment. Can you imagine giving a pet pig your grandmother's beautiful string of expensive pearls? You wouldn't think of it. But every day we give our precious gift of time to people and things in our lives that aren't God's best for us. Discretion and understanding seemed to have escaped us in wise decision making. After all, Mixed Emotions has already invested two years in a dead-end relationship, and who hasn't made a similar mistake? As a young woman, I sure did, spending way too much time with the wrong crowd.

Why Is It So Hard to Make Wise Decisions?

Before we look at how to make the best decisions in these areas, I think it's important to understand what decisions are and what hinders us from making appropriate decisions.

Let's begin with some definitions. Wikipedia.org. defines "decision making" like this:

> Decision making is the cognitive process leading to the selection of a course of action among alternatives. Every decision-making process produces a final choice called a *decision*. It can be an action or an opinion. It begins when we need to do something but we do not know what. Therefore, decision making is a reasoning process which can be rational or irrational, and can be based on explicit assumptions or tactical assumptions.

The Wikipedia entry goes on to reference psychological theorist Isabel Briggs Myers, showing that *feeling; extroversion* and *introversion; judgment* and *perception;* and *sensing* and *intuition* also play a part.[2] To further complicate our decision-making process, as Wikipedia explains, there are common biases that prevent us from feeling that we're making right decisions in our lives. For example, we tend to be willing to gather facts that support certain conclusions but disregard other facts that support different conclusions. In other words, we selectively search for evidence to shore up our beliefs. We believe what we want to believe.

Another problem: we tend to accept the first alternative that looks like it might work for us instead of weighing all the facts. Have you ever told a friend about a problem you were having and, being the friend that she is, she spouted off the first solution that came to her? Being the friend that you are, you immediately accepted it. After all, she's your buddy. But when you got home you had absolutely no peace about the decision, right? We're also creatures of habit with our decisions, unwilling to change thought patterns we've used in the past or to reject what seems unfamiliar.[3] We'll delve more deeply into that in the next chapter.

The list of decision-making problems goes on—like wishful thinking (remember Mixed Emotions?), peer pressure, faulty generalizations . . . you get the idea.

Lest we be hypocritical, who doesn't have a history of bad decisions? I've made plenty of mistakes based on poor or inaccurate information and out-of-whack emotions. A lot of times we will believe what we want to believe whether it's true or not. Obviously, many of us can use some help with this critical investment of time.

The Tough Decisions

As a reporter, I've covered the classic story of bad decisions at home— domestic violence and/or the abusive alcoholic. The wife threatens to leave because she can't take it anymore. She knows she should leave. She knows she doesn't deserve this. But the alcoholic weeps, begs, and pleads. Tells her he'll never swallow another drop of alcohol if only she'll stay. And she makes her decision to stay, because even though she knows he won't quit drinking—because he's said it before—she wants to believe him. This is a bad decision based on false information. And the alcoholic knows he'll drink again, even as he says he won't. The abuser says he will never hit her again, but deep in her heart, she knows the truth. A very difficult, time-stealing, potentially life-stealing decision is made to stay.

As we get older, life throws us through a lot of flaming hoops. One choice will affect another and another, and it goes on and on seemingly forever. While we can change some decisions, there are many others that we're unable to change once we make them. These are extreme cases of tough decisions, because they literally involve someone else's time on this earth (like the case a few years ago of Terri Schiavo and the wide-ranging, ethical controversy and family conflicts surrounding a decision to disconnect her from a life-support system).

There are also other tough decisions we have to make that affect our loved ones and our own time in varying degrees:

- Starting or leaving a relationship that consumes much of your time

- Taking a new job with more pay, but less family time

- Taking a new job with less pay, but more family time

- Choosing to stay at home with children

- Planning for a time in your future (yes, I'm talking about money here)

I'm sure you can think of countless other tough choices. Some people have a difficult time deciding what to wear to work or what to eat for dinner (that would be me). The good news is that we are not alone in this process. The Lord is in the business of ordering our time in big and small ways, if we let him. Bill Robinson, president of

Whitworth University, gave a convocation address at the college in 2004 in which he told this story about a man who makes a huge decision and ends up making history:

> Nehemiah anguished over the blight that had descended on his people and his homeland. When he learned of the Israelites suffering, even the king could not console him.
>
> So Nehemiah the cupbearer, who had the cush job of sampling the king's food and wine, went from fat city to Jerusalem. And there he led his people in the arduous task of rebuilding the city and its walls. Notably, he also used his leadership position to demand social reform. He converted the loan sharks whose extortion-level interest rates stood in the way of most citizens owning property. Nehemiah made history. Jerusalem was rebuilt, and the marks of his labor are borne yet today by Jewish people around the world.
>
> The life of Nehemiah reminds us that when we make history, large or small, our influence can ripple though time in ways we never could have imagined.

History is made and time is invested based on choices. While you may believe that none of your decisions will ever make history for an entire nation, Robinson simplifies the complicated process of making good decisions with this statement:

> I think making history is good, and you should all want to make some. You should be thinking right now about what kind of history you want to make. I think if we thought more about making history we would do better at figuring out the present. But you've got a problem, a big problem. You live in

a culture that tells you every day in every way that life is all about . . . right now. Instant gratification . . .

Ironically, the best way to "make history" is to "think future." . . . The kind of history I want you to consider is the kind you make when somehow your life leaves a broad and enduring mark. What will last after you leave? How will your influence live on? Do you think about that?[4]

Ah, today's decisions made easy. Don't just default to the easy rut answer you've fallen back to again and again. Instead, keep tomorrow in mind. Consider future consequences of this moment's action. Think through the repercussions for you and your loved ones. Take into account your investment of time. Although your decisions may not produce any content for future history books, they are, and will be, affecting you and the people in your life, both now and tomorrow. Decisions we make today will shape our future and our children's futures. One bad choice could eventually leave a lasting imprint on your child's life. No pressure there, right? Fortunately, we can take some comfort in the words of Ann Landers, "Expect trouble as an inevitable part of life and repeat to yourself the most comforting words of all: This too shall pass."[5]

So what's your tough decision today? Are you attempting to make it alone, without guidance from the one who can really give you wisdom?

How will you make your mark through your choices? When we're faced with a really tough decision, how can we quickly and easily come up with a solution? Successful decision making is more than just using analytical skills and intuition. It begins with God's part in giving wisdom and insight, even when our choices don't seem logical. But the quality of our lives will depend on the quality of our decisions, so let me give you a few strategies that have worked for me over the years.

Strategy #1: Simply Ask for Wisdom

How's this for a time-saving solution to the complicated process of decision making? If you remember nothing else from this chapter, remember God promises to give us wisdom when we need it: "If any of you lacks wisdom, let him ask of God, who gives to all generously and without reproach, and it will be given to him" (James 1:5 NASB). As I wrote in my top-ten strategies for the Overwhelmed, meeting with God is first on my list, first thing in the morning. Usually it just involves reading and prayer. But on days when I'm facing an important decision, I'll take God at his Word and ask for his advice and a measure of wisdom that goes beyond my abilities. Seriously. No lofty words or prayers are necessary. It's something like, "Lord, I'm confused. What's the right choice in this matter? Lord, please make this decision very clear to me."

But here's the thing. That's only step one. Step two requires that we actually *believe* the Lord when we read, "But he must ask in faith without any doubting, for the one who doubts is like the surf of the sea, driven and tossed by the wind. For that man ought not to expect that he will receive anything from the Lord, being a double-minded man, unstable in all his ways" (James 1:6–8 NASB).

In other words, let's not waste God's time or ours for that matter. *Don't bother asking God for wisdom if you really don't believe that you'll receive it.* I know it sounds crazy, but when I ask for help

> *God promises to give us wisdom when we need it: "If any of you lacks wisdom, let him ask of God, who gives to all generously and without reproach, and it will be given to him."*
>
> *James 1:5 NASB*

with decisions and actually ask in faith, it's unbelievable what a time saver it is. Maybe not immediately, but sooner than my own striving and stressing can generate, I get an answer. I see more clearly. I suddenly have insight that I didn't have before. And, above all, I have a peace that surpasses my comprehension about the decision. But here's the trap. Once you've asked the Lord for help and believe him for the answer, don't start doubting. Remember how Peter had faith to walk on water when he kept his eyes on Jesus? But once he looked down, he began to sink.

That, of course, takes us to the third part of this strategy—how can we believe in someone we don't know? Getting to know God by spending time with him and by spending time in the Bible will be one of your greatest time savers. He'll keep you out of the traps of life when you choose to know and believe in him. One of my favorite verses is this one: "Trust in the LORD with all your heart, and do not lean on your own understanding. In all of your ways acknowledge Him, and He will make your paths straight" (Proverbs 3:5–6 NASB). How can we acknowledge our ways to him unless we take the time to communicate our plans and concerns to him?

Make this effort, and God will give you new insight into every decision you face. You won't truly understand this until you try it for yourself. He never fails.

Strategy #2: Review Your Mission

As I mentioned earlier, it helps to have a mission statement you can refer to—just one sentence to get you back in focus on what you want to accomplish. As Proverbs 4:26 tells us, "Know where you are headed, and you will stay on solid ground" (CEV).

In making decisions, our job is to remember God's purpose for our lives and make choices that relate to it. Stay in harmony with God's plan and direction. Keep that mission before your eyes.

Write it again here:

Does it feel right to you? Need to make any modifications? Then do so! Then ask these ten simple questions:

10 Ways to Support Your Mission Through Choices

1. Does this decision move me closer to my mission?

2. How could this choice move me away from my mission?

3. Is this decision really mine to make?

4. Am I being distracted by this decision?

5. What do I fear in making this decision?

6. What do I love about making this decision?

7. Who is influencing me in this choice? And why?

8. Have I taken adequate time to pray about this decision?

9. What would Jesus do in this situation?

10. Do I have peace about my decision?

Sometimes his purpose in a specific circumstance or choice is tough to recognize, especially when you have several good options in front of you. Our job is to spot the best choice and recognize the time stealers.

Strategy #3: Define the Real Problem

Dr. Charles Foster, who wrote the book *What Do I Do Now?*[6] participated in a study of people making decisions over a course of twelve years. After the study was complete, he compiled a set of "laws" that should be followed when making important decisions. He says that to begin with, we should focus on the most important thing—the thing that *really* matters. Sometimes this isn't obvious. For example, factors from your background may be smolderingly important, even though now they're lying dormant. They may be the real issue behind other difficulties that are only symptoms. Yet many of us waste time solving problems that aren't the true problem.

This point is also addressed by Mary Ellen Guffey in her book *Business Communication: Process and Product.*[7] She advises us to identify and clarify the problem. The real problem. Your first task is recognizing that a problem exists. Some challenges are big and unmistakable; others may be just continuing annoyances. The first step in reaching a solution is pinpointing the true problem area. On a personal note, we had one child who seemed to be stressed out by school at a very young age. It turned out it had nothing to do with adjusting to classes or homework, as we first thought. She finally confessed the truth that she was being bullied by another little girl who actually hit her. We immediately contacted the school administration, which contacted the parents, and we went into "how to stand up to a bully" role-playing with our daughter. It took quite a bit of time to solve this problem, but at least we were finally dealing with the right problem.

When I feel stymied by life—when I have that niggling feeling that something is wrong—I simply ask God, "What's wrong? What's really wrong?" The answer might come as soon as I've quieted my mind enough to hear it. Or it may take time. Either way, I know that I'll finally be solving the real problem, trusting that God will give me the needed wisdom.

Strategy #4: Dare to Risk

Sometimes we face a choice that's so important, we let fear seep into the equation. We begin imagining the worst that can happen. Before we know it, we've self-talked our way out of what could be a great opportunity. We base our decisions on fear, not facts, and any thought of taking a risk is immediately dismissed. We need to stay where it's safe, right?

A biblical story known as the parable of the talents centers on a man who based his decisions on fear . . . and it cost him, big-time. His boss, before going away, gave a certain amount of money to this man as well as two other employees. The other two went out, made choices, gained information, took risks—and doubled their money, which they gladly reported to the boss when he returned. But the first man's report can only be described as tragic: "Master, I knew you to be a hard man, reaping where you did not sow and gathering where you scattered no seed. And I was afraid, and went away and hid your talent [*piece of silver*] in the ground. See, you have what is yours" (Matthew 25:24–25 NASB).

This employee let his imagination and fear cloud his decision-making ability. As a result, he was punished, and his boss gave his money to the employee who had the most, the one who dared to take a risk. Not fair, you say? Maybe not, but it is the way life works. Isn't it true that the greatest rewards go to the person who isn't afraid to step out of her comfort zone, even a little bit? Doreen Roadman, a financial consultant in many of my stories over the years, says that she wishes "women would take more risks with their money." Yes, failure may be a part of it, but really, which is the greater failure—trying something new or doing nothing at all?

In making decisions, look at the information you have and seek out the information that's still missing. Look for gaps in your knowledge and try either to fill them or take account of them. Once you feel confident that you're basing your decision on facts and not fear, then dare to take a risk.

Strategy #5: Consider Your Sources (Seek Wise Counsel)

The Bible teaches us to seek wise counsel. Would you believe that Uncle Sam agrees? Business.gov ("The Official Business Link to the U.S. Government") posted an article titled "Are You a Good Decision Maker?" It tells us to avoid these particular pitfalls of decision making:

> ▸ *Relying too much on expert information.* People often have a tendency to place too much emphasis on what experts say. Remember, experts are only human and have their own sets of biases and prejudices just like the rest of us. One time, my husband and I trusted our savings to an "expert"

who claimed to know much more than we did about investing. Thousands of dollars lost cured us of ever again simply trusting a self-proclaimed expert without doing our own homework. By seeking information from a lot of different sources, you'll be much better informed than if you focus all your energy on only one source.

> *Overestimating the value of information received from others.* People have a tendency to overestimate the value of certain individuals' advice—such as experts, authority figures, high-status groups, people who seem to have it all together, and people they respect. These people have a way of swaying our opinion simply because we believe they know more than we do. I may love my friend dearly, but she may not be the best one to solve my problems for me. When you find yourself giving away decision-making power to others, ask yourself: Do they know as much about this problem as I do? Are their values the same as mine? Have they had any personal experiences with a problem like mine? In other words, keep their opinions in perspective.

> *Underestimating the value of information received from others.* We also have a tendency to discount or underestimate the information we receive from certain individuals—such as children, low-status groups, the elderly, etc. This is unfortunate, since many times people in these groups can offer a clear perspective on your problem. I have to say, sometimes my children come up with laser-sharp perceptions about family decisions. It's stunning. They see with completely different eyes. My mother and

father are also great sources of wisdom. In other words, these groups may use entirely different values and perceptions in their answers to your questions. The result is a broader perspective of what the issues really are. So if you find yourself discounting the information you receive from anyone, make sure to ask yourself why.[8]

In making decisions, ask yourself: Where did the information come from? How accurate is the information gathered? Is it fact or opinion? Consider your sources carefully.

Strategy #6: Consider Your Biases

Try this exercise: Ask a friend to look around and make note of everything that is green. Now have her close her eyes. Once her eyes are closed, ask her to tell you what around her is red. Most people will not be able to tell you what was red, because they were focusing on what was green.

Our perceptions work the same way. If we have expectations or biases we aren't aware of, we tend to see what we want to see. Likewise, if someone tries to tell us something we don't want to hear, we simply don't hear them.

This is a common mistake many people make. The key is to be aware of your own prejudices and expectations while at the same time staying open to information that comes your way. Does this decision represent various points of view? What biases can be clouding my ability to make a sound decision?

Strategy #7: Consider All Possible Solutions

This is where we get to be creative. Look at possible solutions from every angle you can think of. A problem doesn't have to be solved in the way you usually handle it. Try something new. If you always make the same choices, nothing in life will ever change. You're a visionary in your own life, so be innovative in your decisions.

This is also where analytical skills come into play—the ability to use logic to examine and measure a problem. Your analytical skills can help you examine the ideas and separate the workable ideas from the worthless. Getting analytical can also help you solve *why?* or *should I?* problems when the choices can be tested in

Pretend you're solving the problem for your best friend and see if the answer doesn't become strikingly clear.

terms of facts. For example, which choice works best in terms of my time schedule? Which choice is more efficient?

Earlier I mentioned that solving problems for other people (like Mixed Emotions) is usually much easier than solving our own. That's because we're able to distance ourselves and take the emotion out of the choice. Try doing the same thing in weighing all possible solutions to a tough decision. Pretend you're solving the problem for your best friend, and see if the answer doesn't become strikingly clear.

Strategy #8: Consider the Consequences

One of my favorite authors I've had the chance to interview several times is Dr. Henry Cloud, author of the book *9 Things You Simply Must Do to Succeed in Love and Life*. His work has truly changed the way I live. He says that before you make any decision, "play the movie." In other words, consider all future implications of that decision.[9] Sounds like our Nehemiah story, doesn't it?

Have you ever really stopped to do that? If x, then y; . . . if y happens, then z can happen . . . and so on.

If you're single and considering whom you'll date, what are the future implications of going out with this guy? Does he live the kind of life you would like to live? Does he have the same values?

Tanya is considering getting a second job to pay off her student loans. In playing her movie, she's asking herself: What is the cost in terms of time? How long will it take to pay off my debt if I don't get this job? How long will it take to get on solid financial ground, if I take this job?

Mary is in an abusive marriage. In playing her movie, she's asking herself: What are the consequences for me and the children if I stay in this relationship? Where are the sources of help and support? Is this how I want to spend the rest of my time on this earth?

What are the decisions you're facing now that will affect how your movie turns out? Play it all the way to the very last scene. Do you like what you see? If not, don't waste your valuable time. Don't be another Mixed Emotions.

In his book *Six Thinking Hats*,[10] Edward de Bono describes six colored hats and their roles in business decision making. In wearing one hat, he says to look at all the bad points of the decision. Look at it cautiously and defensively. Try to see why it might not work. This is important because it highlights the weak points in a plan. It allows you to eliminate them, alter them, or prepare contingency plans to counter them. What are the obstacles and how can you best handle them?

To keep from focusing too much on the negative, consider also the positives when playing your movie. Weigh the advantages and disadvantages of each alternative. What are the costs, benefits, and consequences? Most important, which solution best serves your goals?

Again, if there's one hat we need to wear in this process, it's our creative hat.

Strategy #9: Listen to Your Gut (Maybe)

In our hearts, haven't we all wondered this: *Why would the Lord care about my little life when he has a whole universe to run?* Well, the Bible says we are his workmanship, his investment, and he cares deeply about us, down to the smallest details. The very hairs on our heads are *numbered*!

As his workmanship, you have also been given some tools to help you make wise choices. Let's begin with your own God-given intuition. Have you ever made a decision only to have it be followed by a major stomach ache or headache? This is your body talking to you. I'll never forget when we enrolled our youngest daughter in a preschool program that had a great reputation. There was just one problem—I didn't feel great about it. I dropped her off and didn't feel like eating the whole day. Now, you know there's something wrong when that happens to me! Sure enough, our daughter was also unhappy there. The class was too large and too structured. She's the kind of kid who needed to run outside and roll in the dirt a bit. She just didn't fit in at such a young age, so we got her out of there quickly. Funny, my body knew it (my spirit knew it) before my brain would acknowledge it.

Our brains are constantly taking in more information than we can consciously process. All of this extra information gets buried in our subconscious. Although we may not be able to retrieve this information, our bodies store it for us until it is needed. In moments when we need to make a decision, our bodies provide clues to the answer through feelings or gut reactions. Unfortunately, many of us are taught to ignore or bury these feelings.

In addition to your gut instinct, God's Spirit goes beyond your own feelings and physical and emotional reactions. If you ask for wisdom, he'll give you insight and knowledge that you never knew existed. And, remember, he will help you with all your decisions, if you just ask him. This exceeds and outshines your own intuition (which is important). This is actually God's Spirit speaking directly to your spirit.

He'll give you peace that goes beyond all your understanding. The Holy Spirit is described as the Comforter, and he'll provide that comfort in the choices you have to make. This type of wisdom may not happen overnight. Then again, it may. Either way, slow down and quiet your mind before making any final decision. Don't decide until you're ready. We think we have to act quickly in this push-and-shove era of cell phones and email. But patience is not only a virtue; it's a great decision-making strategy.

Strategy #10: Act on Your Decisions

As each year passes and life seems to get harder, do you ever long for those times when decisions were already made for you? What you ate and drank, when you went to bed, which school you went to—these decisions were all handled for you.

Guess what? Those years are over. Now we have the opportunity to create our own lives. To innovate. To shape our existence along new lines. To step beyond the fear of acting on our decisions. Harriet Beecher Stowe once said, "I long to put the experience of fifty years at once into your young lives. To give you at once the key to that treasure chamber every gem of which has cost me tears and struggles and prayers, but you must work for these inward treasures yourselves.[11]

Another historical woman had to own her decisions in a society that wasn't as kind to women as ours. After considering her field of investment—taking time and meditating upon her choice—the very capable and astute businesswoman in Proverbs 31 then took action. She stepped through the fear and purchased her field of dreams, an investment that she went on to improve and which would provide income for her family for years to come. In the same way, we can make a decision and put it into action. Just like her, we follow through on our decisions by monitoring the results of implementing our plan.

We've all had to face tough decisions that would ultimately change the course of our own futures and our children's futures. Once you've made a decision, don't waste time by second-guessing yourself. We don't have to be like a wave driven and tossed by the sea. Your decisions will impact your greatest asset on this earth, time, so choose wisely and in peace.

ACTION APPLICATION
Moving Forward

Choose just one decision you've been putting off (perhaps for years). Write it here:

Go through the ten-strategy plan for decision making and write out an action step to take for each one:

Strategy #1: Simply Ask for Wisdom
Complete this prayer: Dear God, I need . . .

Strategy #2: Review Your Mission
Rewrite your Mission Statement here:

My decision does/[doesn't] work with my Mission Statement. Why?

Strategy #3: Define the Real Problem

ACTION APPLICATION

Strategy #4: Dare to Risk
I'm afraid of . . .

Strategy #5: Consider Your Sources (Seek Wise Counsel)
Here are three people I can ask about this issue . . .

Strategy #6: Consider Your Biases
I think this is blocking me from the best solution:

Strategy #7: Consider All Possible Solutions
Here are three different ideas on how to resolve this:

ACTION APPLICATION

Strategy #8: Consider the Consequences
If I make my decision, and play my movie, it will affect me and my loved ones by . . .

Strategy #9: Listen to Your Gut (Maybe)
I think my heart is telling me to . . .

Strategy #10: Act on Your Decisions
My first step to act on my decision will be to . . .

My second step to act on my decision will be to . . .

Consciously do the very thing you've been afraid of . . . and watch your fear evaporate.

Won't it feel good to get this burden off your mind for good?

6

The Self-Stressed

10 Smart Strategies Using Thoughts and Words

*Be transformed by the renewing of your mind, so that you may prove
what the will of God is, that which is good and acceptable and perfect.*

—ROMANS 12:2 NASB

Ten + Ten = Time

10 Smart Strategies Using Thoughts and Words

Strategy #1: Realize That Someday Is Today.

Strategy #2: Remember Who You Are.

Strategy #3: Own the Power of Your Thoughts.

Strategy #4: Challenge Automatic Thinking.

Strategy #5: Monitor Your Words for One Day.

Strategy #6: Replace Derailer Words.

Strategy #7: Wasted Words, Wasted Time.

Strategy #8: Embrace the Most Powerful Word.

Strategy #9: Embrace Failure as a Time Teacher.

Strategy #10: Outrun a Lesser Version of Yourself.

NOTE FROM GOD

> *My Dearest Self-Stressed Daughter:*
>
> *I have an idea for you. Instead of fretting and worrying about everyone and everything you want to accomplish, how about coming to me? How about shaping your worries into prayers, letting me know your concerns? Before you know it, a sense of my wholeness, of everything coming together for good, will come and settle you down. It will be wonderful. You'll see. I have another idea for you as well, my Self-Stressed beloved. You'll live a happier, more peaceful life if you focus on things that are true, noble, reputable, authentic, compelling, gracious—the best, not the worst; the beautiful, not the ugly; things to praise, not things to speak negatively about. Do this, even in times of trouble, and I promise that everything will work together, according to my excellent harmony.*
>
>

Love always,

God
>

(Inspired by Philippians 4:4–8 MSG)

We've talked a lot about attitude and outcome in terms of time. But what about those days when no amount of positive thinking will solve our problems? What about when life is really, really awful and time traps sap us of energy and joy for the things that really matter? Our Self-Stressed women said they were "worrying about too many things"; "under a lot of stress"; "trying to accomplish too much at once." Some were suffering from chronic illness or physical or emotional pain. Others were mourning a death or dealing with divorce or separation. Many, though, were not suffering such major, sudden life-altering disruptions. They were simply living "ordinary" lives with their accompanying challenges. Have you ever heard yourself say the same things these women wrote us?

"Worrying about too many things in my life"

"Lack of focus"

"Completely unorganized and under a lot of stress"

"Trying to accomplish too much at once"

Hearing a platitude like "just try to think nice thoughts" isn't going to solve these problems. It's easy to feel successful and positive when things are going well, but an important factor in a successful life involves making it through the tough times. But how do you do it? How do you stay positive when life goes sour?

In many ways, life was agonizing for the apostle Paul. Here he was, trying to do a good thing and getting beaten up at every turn. Listen to his description of the ordeals he went through:

Are they servants of Christ? I know I sound like a madman, but I have served him far more! I have worked harder, been put in prison more often, been whipped times without number, and faced death again and again. Five different times the Jewish leaders gave me thirty-nine lashes. Three times I was beaten with rods. Once I was stoned. Three times I was shipwrecked. Once I spent a whole night and a day adrift at sea. I have traveled on many long journeys. I have faced danger from rivers and from robbers. I have faced danger from my own people, the Jews, as well as from the Gentiles. I have faced danger in the cities, in the deserts, and on the seas. And I have faced danger from men who claim to be believers but are not. I have worked hard and long, enduring many sleepless nights. I have been hungry and thirsty and have often gone without food. I have shivered in the cold, without enough clothing to keep me warm. (2 Corinthians 11:23–27 NLT)

Perhaps you feel like Paul did, working at your job or dealing with your problems! Or maybe his struggles put yours into perspective. Either way, let's just agree that life is hard sometimes.

But listen to how Paul responded *in spite of* these unpleasant circumstances:

Summing it all up, friends, I'd say you'll do best by filling your minds and meditating on things true, noble, reputable, authentic, compelling, gracious—the best, not the worst; the beautiful, not the ugly; things to praise, not things to curse. Put into practice what you learned from me, what you heard and saw and realized. Do that, and God, who makes everything work together, will work you into his most excellent harmonies. (Philippians 4:8–9 MSG)

Paul shows us exactly how he overcame, how he continued to run the race no matter what happened. It was all in his head and his heart. Relying on the power of the Holy Spirit, he kept a positive attitude. He reminds me of one of my favorite guests on our show, *Living the Life*. When Jennifer Rothschild was just fifteen years old, she lost her sight to a rare, degenerative eye disease. But she never lost her joy for life, and today she tells her story through books and music, speaking encouragement to women around the nation. The apostle James also tells us to choose to think *joyously* when we face trials and challenges in life:

> Consider it a sheer gift, friends, when tests and challenges come at you from all sides. You know that under pressure, your faith-life is forced into the open and shows its true colors. So don't try to get out of anything prematurely. Let it do its work so you become mature and well-developed, not deficient in any way. (James 1:2–3 MSG)

You may not *feel* that your current situation is a gift or like celebrating the tough time you're in. But haven't there been hard times in your past that actually had a good impact on your personality or your character growth? In the long run of events, haven't you seen rich benefits that could be attributed directly to times of struggle or suffering? One way to get through a tough time with a positive spirit is to remember those words of James *during* the problem, not just in hindsight.

Many of the stumbling blocks that our Self-Stressed encounter can be attributed to a misuse of thoughts or words. So for you, my stressed-out sis, here are ten strategies to help you overcome the internal time traps that can rob us all of years.

Strategy #1: Realize That Someday Is Today

Self-Stressed friends, take a moment and think about why you picked up this book. Most likely because there is something or someone (maybe you) robbing you of time and joy. But you also sense there is an answer, don't you? You've probably thought about your future.

Dreamed about it. Who hasn't? And whenever someone mentions the future, an image pops unbidden into your mind. From starting your own family to starting your own business. From renting a home to mustering up the courage (and the dollars) to buy your first.

Whatever your dream, "someday" dips and sways at the edge of your mind, inspiring and exhilarating. Dreams are the easy part. The more difficult part involves navigating the path and staying the course to fulfilling your dreams, no matter what storms may blow in. But I'm here to tell you, Self-Stressed ladies, someday is today. Remember, this book is not about mastering a to-do list. *Our satisfaction with time spent is linked with how we feel about our investment of minutes and days, not in how much we actually accomplish.* Are we spending our time working toward our goals, even in baby steps?

Review your stated goals (page 55) and mission statement (page 51) and put your top three goals down again here, and then list 1 to 3 baby steps you could do this month, this week—or even better—today, to get closer to them!

GOAL	BABY STEP(S)
1.	
2.	
3.	

Many of us will fill in those blanks and then immediately think, *no way.* Our survey showed that *internal* factors were huge in trapping time and keeping us from our goals and dreams, especially for Self-Stressed women who said attitude, stress, and disorganization were preventing them from better time management. I want to hug the woman who wrote, "There's just too much stress and not enough time and too much to do and not enough money to do everything I want to do. I have no time!" I certainly understand. Been there. Felt that.

Other internally pressured women we surveyed said that worry, lack of motivation, lack of interest, and feelings of being over-whelmed prevented them from better managing their time and reaching their dreams. So here's the question, ladies: how much meditation do we give to our own meditations? In other words, are we actually aware of our thoughts, positive or negative? And are we aware that our thoughts can completely change the direction of our lives? Dr. Henry Cloud, one of my favorite guests already mentioned, came on our show to talk about his alternative book to the bestseller *The Secret*. In *The Secret Things of God*, Henry confirms that "what happens inside your head will find it's way outside—into your life."[1]

So let's talk about what's going on in our heads. Again, I'm no therapist, but I do know the best Counselor of all—the Lord. The Bible teaches us to take every thought captive for Christ: "We break down every thought and proud thing that puts itself up against the wisdom of God. We take hold of every thought and make it obey Christ" (2 Corinthians 10:5 NLV). That means our battle is with every negative thought, big or small. But what does it mean to take our thoughts captive for Christ?

First it implies a conscious reliance on God's power and help; his strength is the only thing that makes our victory possible. Our thoughts, in and of themselves, are not sovereign. In fact, they can be dead wrong. God is the only one who is sovereign.

Second, it means that with his guidance we learn to recognize our time-wasting thoughts and words, refute the negatives, and replace those disempowering images with life-giving thoughts that are consistent with the truth found in God's holy, life-transforming Word. Again, he is the one who created you in the first place, and he knows the best plan for your life. His thoughts are supreme, so why not tap into that power to transform how you view yourself and your abilities?

Strategy #2: Remember Who You Are

Here are a few questions: Who do you believe you are? What thoughts do you allow into your mind about yourself? Do you understand that you are valued, treasured, and uniquely created by God, who is still intimately involved in every detail of your life? The Bible says you are fearfully and wonderfully made. And did you know that in God's eyes, you're royalty? I'm not kidding! If you've accepted Jesus into your life, you've been adopted into his family. You're a child of the King.

A shift took place in the way I saw myself and my place in the world when I quit trying to figure things out by myself. I began submitting my thoughts to God on a daily basis by meeting with him first thing in the morning, so he could help me sort out my time traps. As I mentioned, on days that I'm "too busy," or when I've hit the snooze button one too many times and I miss this meeting, I invariably flounder. God uses this morning meeting to help me order my schedule and my thoughts. On these days, I clearly know who I am in Christ. Just like you, I am God's child (see John 1:12); I've been redeemed and forgiven (see Colossians 1:13–14); I'm complete in Christ (see Colossians 2:9–10).[2]

One author I interviewed, Hayley DiMarco, calls it "God esteem" as opposed to self-esteem. She says that God-esteem means seeing ourselves through his eyes, as the beloved and cherished children we are. Slowly I've come to realize that every day is a cause for celebration, that time itself is a gift. It didn't happen overnight, but that's to be expected. I'd spent a very long time on autopilot, allowing my inner thoughts to derail everything I wanted to do and believe. Ignoring them took a monumental effort, but it has allowed me to carefully and more realistically weigh the value of investing my time.

Strategy #3: Own the Power of Your Thoughts

Once you recognize who you are in God, it's important to recognize the power of your own mental processes in achieving or derailing your success. This became very clear to me one day on the job as a reporter. As part of my media role, sometimes I have to memorize large amounts of material to say it into the camera in a conversational way. That particular day everything was going wrong. Technical problems, people problems, me problems. Ironically, as I let anger and irritation creep into my mind, my memory was blocked. In order to get the job done, I had no choice but to release the negative thoughts and focus. When I did, the words flowed. Wow! How much time and effort would I save if I applied that principle to the rest of my life?

The great news is that God understands what's going on in our heads and loves us anyway. David writes:

> O LORD, you have searched me and you know me. You know when I sit and when I rise; you perceive my thoughts from

afar. You discern my going out and my lying down; you are familiar with all my ways. Before a word is on my tongue you know it completely, O Lord. (Psalm 139:1–4 NIV)

Guess what? We haven't been hiding anything from God. He already knows all the "what ifs" and worries in our minds. If we choose to be honest with him about how we feel and what we're afraid of, he'll give us the power to take a step in the right direction.

The most successful people I've interviewed have taught me that fear dissolves when you take action . . . even little baby steps. Do you know why that's true? Because fear is a thought process that feeds on stagnation. Mentally sitting still allows you to dwell on the discouraging "could haves" and "might haves" rather than focusing on what is. When you know where you're going, when you have a plan and a course of action, there isn't time to think about what should have been. The excitement of chasing the future propels you into the next phase and the next process, filling your mind with life-enriching potential. There just isn't room to bother with the rest.

Making things happen is 88 percent attitude and 12 percent education, according to a Stanford Research Institute study. Also in her article "Positive Attitude—Enough Already," author Christine Corelli notes that companies want people who hunger for challenges, are flexible to change, and possess a positive, uplifting attitude in the work environment.[3] If the top corporations are looking for that attitude to drive their businesses forward, doesn't it follow that having that same mind-set in your life will drive you to success in whatever dream you're hoping to realize?

For some people it's nearly impossible to believe that just thinking positive thoughts can change so much in their lives. But studies have shown this to be true, to the point that doctors have been known to give out instructions for "play" to cancer patients as readily as prescriptions for painkillers. A positive attitude is linked to a healthy heart, longer life, and a myriad of other benefits.

Organizations like the Make-A-Wish Foundation focus all of their energy on creating happy, positive trips for critically ill children, making these vacations completely painless for the entire family in order to strengthen the hearts and minds of the children. And in research done by the University of Texas with more than 1,500 older men and women, those with positive, life-affirming attitudes were found to be less likely to get frail and sick in their older years than those who were more pessimistic.[4] Realizing our future wishes and dreams comes first from submitting today's thoughts and actions to the Lord daily. Hope gives the motivation to try again, which may be what we're missing as Self-Stressed ladies.

Negative Thoughts versus Positive Thoughts

How does your internal monologue go? Which words begin the sentences?

NEGATIVE	POSITIVE
I can't . . .	*I can* . . .
I don't . . .	*I do* . . .
I won't . . .	*I will* . . .
I'm not . . .	*I am* . . .
I couldn't . . .	*I could* . . .

Strategy #4: Challenge Automatic Thinking

Unfortunately, many of us still suffer from teen angst well into adulthood. It's automatic. The little girl who once thought she could grow up to be president of the United States is now plagued with doubt. If we're honest, most of our emotional responses tend toward the negative, and fear often replaces hope and faith. The immediate reaction to almost any situation usually involves finding the worst-case scenario and obsessing about it.

Psychologists have a term for this immediate response: *automatic thinking*.[5] It means that the thoughts come completely without reason or forethought. They're habitual. There's nothing inherently bad about having automatic responses. This internal "noise" is a running commentary of how we see ourselves and our lives. The more negative our internal noise, the less we tend to think of ourselves. It then follows that the more positive our internal noise, the higher our self-esteem—and our level of happiness—will be.

Okay, so the internal noise is there, and it's dragging us down. What do we do about it? I mean, it's in our heads so it's not like we can ignore it, right?

Chances are we can't. Instead, do just the opposite. Focus on what's being said by those voices in your head. Pay attention like you never have before. Zero in on what kinds of thoughts are keeping you back from reaching your potential; write them down, then replace those lies with the truth. Challenge that automatic thinking. Fight those nagging doubts! For example, every time you think, *There's no way I will ever reach this goal,* immediately think, *Why not? I know my stuff as well as anyone, and I have the added edge of doing it better. I know I can do the job, and I know I'm the best person for it. God, thank you for this challenge; strengthen me to do it well, to your glory.* Try it. It works!

Success doesn't come by making negative statements, no matter how warranted they may be. For those who work outside the home, take a look at the peacocks you know who seem to waltz up the corporate ladder with nary a ruffled feather. Or think about the women who seem to make friends everywhere they go. What is it that makes these people successful? If you look closely—past your own frustration or (gasp!) jealousy—you'll see it. Successful people make great efforts to be comfortable with whatever situation arises. It's automatic. They turn the ugly scenarios into times of learning and growth, rather than a time to lock and load. Every day they show up ready to see what the day will bring them, hair carefully coifed, with an attitude as well-tended as their wardrobe. These people have a mind-set that doesn't leave room for bemoaning the current state of affairs.

Life-coach trainer Karman Morey believes there's a strong correlation between being able to keep a positive mental picture and experiencing success in life. He conducted a study of positive and negative thinkers, using personal interviews and observing what is happening every day. He found many things that positive thinkers had in common:

It is about choice in emotional response. People with this ability choose their own focus regardless of the circumstance. They tend to remain in a resourceful state, and make the most of whatever life offers them. Having choice in their attitude and focus allows them to "Seize the Day," create good memories, and project a positive future. They solve problems as quickly as possible. They often do more, go further, and experience more enjoyable, fulfilling, and satisfying lives.[6]

Those whom Morey interviewed said the most useful emotion they had in their arsenal was gratitude; they found something to be grateful for despite unhappy periods of time.

Here again, it helps to analyze what successful people, like Jennifer Rothschild, do. The automatic thinking of successful people has a constructive, positive theme. These folks routinely trust God for their success, in his plan, such that there's no reason to doubt. They don't squabble about *what ifs* or *whys*. Instead they focus on the *how* and *when*. Think about someone who is like Jennifer in your life—someone whose automatic thinking revolves around success rather than failure, thus creating a history of accomplishments to reinforce their positive inner dialogue. What a lovely cycle to be in the midst of!

We need to adjust our automatic internal dialogue to one that reaffirms what we *should* be thinking of ourselves. Be nice to yourself while you work on this transformation. Chances are pretty high that you'll make mistakes, have bad days, and occasionally think that none of the effort is worth it. Stick with it and try not to be too hard on yourself. The best place to start every day is the truth found in God's Word. We've all heard this verse: "You will know the truth, and the truth will set you free" (John 8:32 NIV). Jesus is talking about holding fast to his teachings in order to be free from our old, destructive lifestyles, letting his Word and Spirit soak our lives and minds to become our thoughts. It's amazing what happens when we take time to hear what God says about our lives. In time, our new way of thinking will become our new *automatic* thinking!

Replace Derailer Thoughts

Here's how you can shift your mind into a more uplifting direction:

I spend much of my time stressing out.—**"The Lord created me and understands what I'm going through. He will provide the power and peace to overcome my challenges, if I ask him." (from James I and Philippians 4:6–7)**

I can't get motivated.—**"I can do all things through Christ giving me the strength." (from Philippians 4:13)**

I spend my time worrying about the future.—**"God has plans for me and my future. I am his child, and he wants the best for me and my family." (from Jeremiah 29:11)**

I can't do what I want with my time because I can't afford it.—**"God has promised to supply all of my needs, if I ask him for help. Together, we can find some creative ways to afford the life I want." (from Philippians 4:19)**

Why would the Lord give me the time of day?—**"I am so important to the Lord that he gave his only precious Son to die for me. His time on this earth was spent for me." (from John 3:16)**

There are many things in life that offer few or no choices, but the way you think isn't one of them. You have a choice every waking moment of every day about how you see the life you lead. Your thoughts are an investment of your time every day. Make the choice to think beneficial thoughts and to believe what God says about you!

Strategy #5: Monitor Your Words for One Day

Speaking of what's going on in our heads, let's talk about the words we use and our investment of time. Does this really make a difference in achieving what matters to us? Consider Lisa and Lauren who were applying for the same job. Their resumes reflected similar backgrounds and experience, and the company's human resources director invited each for an interview.

As Lisa got ready, she had some negative internal dialogue going on, telling herself not to get her hopes up because she wasn't going to get the job anyway. They wouldn't like the way she dressed or how she answered questions. She looked at her past experience with job interviews and knew she didn't do well in those situations.

Sitting across from the interviewer, Lisa was nervous and uncomfortable, often stumbling through her answers. When asked if she could handle certain tasks, she suggested that she probably could do it even though it was new to her. She looked around nervously instead of making eye contact with the interviewer. Why bother? This interview was just a waste of time. The outcome was inevitable, right?

Sadly, Lisa had talked herself into failure before she even walked through the door.

Lauren's interview went a bit differently. She told herself that she was the perfect person for the job. In fact, during the meeting, she felt she was there to interview this company as her prospective employer, rather than the other way around. She used words to communicate her strengths clearly, and she asked specific questions about the company's operation, which showed that she'd done her research and knew a great deal about this business. She told the interviewer that she would make a strong contribution as a member of the team and felt eager to demonstrate her potential. Lauren would welcome new challenges and use her ability to solve problems and motivate people in order to get the job done.

Can you guess who got the job? Both Lisa and Lauren were qualified. They had similar educations and the same number of years of experience. The biggest difference between them was evident in the way they communicated their self-confidence or, in Lisa's case, the lack thereof.

Lisa accepts failure because she creates and listens to her own doubts. The words *can't* and *won't* are so ingrained into her thought patterns that they overflow into her life experiences. We know that language is a powerful tool. "People can get many good things by the words they say" (Proverbs 12:14, *The Book*). For just a moment, think about the words you speak to yourself. Eventually, this language will spill over into your relationships with others. How many times have you grumbled about someone else getting the break that *you* should have had? Why subject yourself to this pain when you have the power to prevent it? Just for one day, record the number of times you speak a negative word to yourself or someone else. How is this negativity impacting your time with others and your overall quality of life?

Strategy #6: Replace Derailer Words

"Words satisfy the soul as food satisfies the stomach; the right words on a person's lips bring satisfaction" (Proverbs 18:20, *The Book*). That means words can also work for us and our investment of time here on this earth. But how many times have you heard yourself making statements like, "I'm not as good as everyone else," or, "I'm a woman, so they won't listen to me," or, "Nothing ever changes"? If you keep telling yourself you can't achieve something—because you're not intelligent enough, talented enough, or fortunate enough—nothing anyone else says is going to make a difference. Success begins from inside, with that little voice that tells you, *Yes, I can.*

John Vestman is a music engineer and offers motivation to musicians, but his advice is relevant to anyone, with or without an instrument. He suggests you phrase your desires in terms of what you want instead of what you don't want. Instead of, "I'm broke and I don't have enough money to buy that guitar," he suggests replacing the thought with, "I'm working on increasing my income so I can afford a new guitar." Vestman recommends this strategy for talking to children. As an example, say, "Stay here on the sidewalk where you'll be safe" instead of, "Don't run into the street—you'll get hit by a car." Vestman adds that if you do say a negative, then "just follow it with a positive."[7]

In the same way we tend to think automatically, we also fall into the trap of speaking by rote. We're so conditioned to react in negative ways following the path of our negative words. Our everyday language reinforces this way of thinking: *dead tired, scraping by, flat broke, ugly as sin, bad habits, terrible twos, sick and tired, not guilty* (why not say "innocent"?), and *dumb blonde*. Two-year-olds aren't necessarily terrible, nor are blondes, as a rule, less intelligent than the rest of the population. For every bad example, you can find a good one. You just have to look for it, and far too often it's easier to accept the negative. But easy is not always best.

Here's a challenge for you. The next time you hear someone spout a negativism like "There's no way we can get there on time," counter it with positive words: "Let's do our best and see if we can make it." Do this with your own negative thoughts as well. Treat the "bad talk" with a dose of positive speaking. Instead of "I'm such an idiot," tell yourself, "Well, I slipped up; that makes me human, not stupid." When you're tempted to say, "Nothing is going right in my life," try saying, "I'm healthy and happy." Why not replace "I'll never understand how to do this" with "I'll work hard, and with God's help I'll master this task." Instead of "No one understands" or "No one loves me," emphatically state, "I am fully loved and accepted by the God of the universe!" Take that, negative words!

While we may not think of them as negative, even some of our common phrases can be subtle downers for us and the people to whom we say them. So think about the words you use. Jot down a list of some of your common phrases.

Here are some of mine: "I don't have time." "I don't feel like it." "Can't we find something better to watch?" And "We can't afford that." They'd be better said as, "I will find and schedule the time, if this is something that matters to me." "I will choose to invest my time elsewhere." "Let's find something to watch that is a better use of our time." "Through God's resources and our creativity, we will find a way to afford that."

Sound better? A similar language blooper is the answer "I don't know." *I don't know* says the issue ends right here. You don't know the answer and you don't care. In the working world especially, a customer or supervisor will not be pleased by this type of quick dismissal. While it may be a perfectly accurate answer, the better response is to say, "I'm not sure of the answer, but I'll find out." Again, switch from the negative to the positive.

Negative responses are easy! It takes more effort to phrase things in a positive light, but if you do, the ultimate result is a boost for both you and the person you're addressing.

Try to put yourself in the shoes of the person listening to you. Wouldn't the positive versions of your common phrases just make you feel better? Now you try it.

Strategy #7: Wasted Words, Wasted Time

"If you keep your mouth shut, you will stay out of trouble" (Proverbs 21:23 *THE BOOK*). Yes, the Bible really says that! And here's another warning about how we use words, "Those who love to talk will experience the consequences, for the tongue can kill or nourish life" (Proverbs 18:21, *THE BOOK*).

Della Menechella is a speaker, author, and trainer who helps people achieve greater success. She says the key is to remove negative words and thoughts. "Words create feelings and feelings impact behavior," she says. "It is almost impossible to act positively when you use negative words. If you use limiting words, you will act in a corresponding manner, because we always act the way we describe ourselves." Menechella describes negative speech as complaints, gossip, whining, and grumbling. People talk about how crummy life is. "Then," she notes, "they wonder why their lives are not filled with joy and success. While it might seem like a good idea to regularly talk about things that bother you, you pay a huge price for it."[8]

Are we wasting time—years in some cases—because of careless words? Effective, time-enhancing communication comes from stringing words together and delivering them so that the message is direct and conveys what we really mean. Jesus never wasted a word. On the other hand, have you ever listened while someone goes through a verbal windup? It goes something like this: "I need to ask you something, and it's okay if you say no because I know you're, like, really, really busy, but . . . um . . . I was thinking, you know, and I talked to my neighbor about this, too, when he was over the other day, you know, when you went to do those errands, and, well, he was totally in agreement, so we thought that if you agreed, too, that would be great, but, like I said, you know, you can say no if you can't do it . . ." Is this effective communication, or wasted words and wasted time? I think we know the answer. Here's a massive time saver for all of us: Think before we speak. If you're not sure how to phrase a request or a statement, pause. Think about it. Avoid the pointless windup long enough to gather a simple string of effective words.

Take it from an old TV person: If you really want to learn how *not* to waste words, read an ad or listen to a commercial. Check out a billboard. Those roadside ads are written so someone driving by at fifty miles per hour will be able to get the message. The television and advertising communities use language intended for a fifth-grade reading level, but they use this vocabulary creatively, persuasively, and effectively. Every word has value. Ad writers don't waste words, because they realize that only a small minority of people are willing to read more than they have to. One of the most successful advertising campaigns in the past decade is just two words: "Got milk?"

Too many words can waste time, and so can *weak* words. If an advertiser wants you to try a new drink, it won't say, "Take a sip of our beverage and you might like it." Would this convince you to give it a shot? No way. Instead, the ad copywriter picks words that deliver the strongest message, without any waste. No lengthy pleas. They have your attention for only a moment, and they have to deliver a solid hit. What if the makers of Coke said, "It's close to the real thing?" Or Avis advertised, "We hope to try harder," or NBC tried to captivate you with, "Might-possibly-want-to-see TV." You get the idea. If the writers didn't understand the value of the words, the ads would be dull and ineffective.

There's also nothing noncommittal about advertising language. Buy this and you *will* feel better, lose weight, love the taste, look great, be healthier, or otherwise experience a significant advantage over your current existence. There's no "maybe" or even the slightest hint of doubt. The job of advertising is to communicate confidence in whatever the ad is selling in order to convince you to give it a try. They focus on three fundamental benefits to the consumer: save time, save money, improve your lifestyle. That's it. These are the basic motives for making the decision to use a product or service.

In reviewing press releases for guests who want to be on our program, I usually make my determination by the first few words or the first sentence. Word power translates to airtime. Also, I've often referred to writing and speaking as low-fat endeavors. Think of each word as being a glob of fat. Rather than plop down these weighted phrases and thoughts, trim the fat. Why use two or three words when one good one will do a better job? Instead of "drove quickly" use "sped." Remember, Jesus changed lives and changed the world with two simple words: "Follow me."

So why not use your language in the same way to add value to your life and save time? You don't need to tell a prospective employer that you *think* your qualifications are a good match. Be confident. You're *certain* your qualifications are an *excellent* match. You *will* be a valuable addition to the staff. If you have any doubt, don't let it show. You aren't just responsible for handling a task; you *manage, direct,* or *implement* it.

Like advertising copywriters, motivational speakers make a living through their powerful use of language. They reach out to their audiences and reel them in by digging into their toolkits and skillfully selecting strong words, which they deliver with confidence. "You *will* succeed if you believe in yourself"—not "you might succeed" or "you could succeed." There are no ifs, ands, or buts here. They make the declaration. By consciously using language to make it more powerful and positive, they inspire others to find similar energy and drive within themselves. Persuasive, encouraging, and stimulating language is infectious.

Think positively and speak your ideas with confidence. Find words that encourage, support, and motivate your friends, family, and coworkers. Select words that have power and energy, and avoid those that fizzle out. Don't use long sentences when you can deliver the idea with a few words. When you want to be persuasive, take a lesson from the advertising world. "Just do it."

Testing Your Words

Do you remember those school assignments when your teacher demanded an essay of 250 words about your summer vacation? *I had a very, very, very fun summer that was really, really, really great.* You'd write the sentence, then stop and count the words. Right? Back then, you probably didn't have enough words in your toolbox to make an interesting composition. At least, that's what you thought.

To begin investing time in more positive, life-affirming words, begin with the written word. Sit in front of a computer or pick up a pen and just write a letter to God about what you want to accomplish this next year. Write to God as if you were speaking to another person (which you are). Don't worry about the punctuation, grammar, or spelling. Just get the ideas on the page. No one will read your letter except you, so the pressure of being judged is gone.

Now look at the words you're choosing. Are they moving you closer to your dreams and goals, or are they simply wasting your time? Can you cut out extraneous or meaningless words? What's the *heart* of what you're trying to say?

Strategy #8: Embrace the Most Powerful Word

You wouldn't fire up a chainsaw without having some instruction (hopefully), and you wouldn't use a sledgehammer to pound a nail into a wall. Think about the damage you might cause! So if you're going to tackle your language challenges, start by learning how your communication tools work by learning from the Source. We don't need a degree in English or a massive vocabulary to improve our effectiveness with words. We do, however, need God's Word in our lives and the power of the Holy Spirit to transform our speaking and thinking from a pit of despair into a well of life. Just as if you were trying to learn a new language, such as French or Spanish, invest time in learning the language of your Creator. Remember, Jesus never wasted a word.

The Bible begins with God literally speaking life into existence: "God said, 'Let there be light'; and there was light" (Genesis 1:3 NASB). Jesus is referred to as the living Word: "In the beginning was the Word, and the Word was with God, and the Word was God" (John 1:1 NASB). It's by this Word, through the power of the Holy Spirit, that we can speak hope, healing, and abundant life to ourselves and others.

I can't stress enough the difference this has made in my own life. One of my own little goals is to memorize three verses of Scripture most weeks. I want his Word to already be in my head on those days when I'm stressing out and find myself steeped in negative self-talk. His Word then replaces my word, which leads to a completely different outcome.

Strategy # 9: Embrace Failure as a Time Teacher

Everyone faces a time in life when she looks at how she's spending her time and thinks, *How did I get here and is this what I really want?*

It happened to me. One day it dawned on me that somewhere along the way I'd taken a wrong turn. The problem wasn't in my life, but rather in how I saw my life. I could have stopped right there and given in to depression because of mistakes I'd made and the time I'd wasted giving in to negative thoughts. But I made a different choice. I decided to start fresh and get back on the path I really wanted to travel. I chose to renew my commitment to God and refocus on my goals instead of obsessing on my failures.

As I mentioned, negative thoughts and words may often have their root in fear of failure. Perhaps out of self-preservation, insecurity, or pride, we fear taking a chance. In our worries and nightmares, we obsess about the possibility of failing. Well, what would really happen if you do? I've never seen a study where failure was listed as one of the leading causes of death in this or any other country. The absolute worst that will happen is that someone can say, "I told you so." Believe me, it's much better to hear the I-told-you-sos than it is to wake up one day and realize that you never took a chance. The best inventors in the world fail hundreds of times before finding the right combination or design!

Successful people look beyond the here and now to focus on where they're going and how they're going to get there. Having this type of perspective helps us bounce back from setbacks and correct our course when we run astray, rather than remain stuck in time-stripping eddies in the river.

Even something like financial failure doesn't mean much if you can still see the road ahead. One of the most successful and popular businessmen around today once faced total financial ruin. Donald Trump built an empire on catering to the rich and famous. He bought, renovated, and sold sumptuous properties during the 1980s. His name became synonymous with opulence—until everything came crashing down around his ears in a real-estate market collapse. By 1990, Trump had acquired a personal debt of more than $900 million and business debt exceeding $3.5 million. Amazingly, he paid off all this debt within four years. Four years!

Trump rallied, and within ten years he came back with an even bigger portfolio than before. He's become a household name through his reality television series, *The Apprentice*. This amazing feat came from hard work and refusing to give up in the middle of the game. His attitude is one of moving forward, not wallowing in the past. He's quoted as saying, "I try to learn from the past, but I plan for the future by focusing exclusively on the present. That's where the fun is."[9]

So why let minor—or major—thoughts and inconveniences stop you from doing what you want to do? Not everyone wants to run a multibillion-dollar enterprise, but even those content with a lemonade stand have to believe that their drink will be the best and the most in demand on the block in order to sell a single cup. With that belief comes the strength to get out there and make it happen. Can you make it to the end result? You can if you truly believe you can. You may not take the most direct route, or the most convenient one, but eventually you can get there. Plug along even when you don't feel like it. Learn from your mistakes and continue to move upward and onward no matter what. For all successful people you can think of, there have been times in their lives when they did not feel up to the challenge. The difference between them and those who failed is what thoughts they allowed into their minds when all seemed lost.

So here's the point: in most cases, life is longer than our daily troubles. It might take awhile before we reach our goals, and there may be bumps along the way. But there's more life to live after we make a mistake, so we have to choose how we're going to use the rest of our time. Will we sit down and wallow in our failure? Or believe in ourselves and keep fighting for our dreams? The choice is entirely our own. Now is the time to face three of your most disempowering thoughts or words and take action to replace them.

*My Top 3 Goal-Halting Errors
and The Alternative Belief I Must Adopt
To Combat Them:*

Disempowering Belief	Alternative Belief
1.	
2.	
3.	

Strategy #10: Outrun a Lesser Version of Yourself

Successful people have a way about them that draws you in. It stems from their inner strength, their confidence, and their desire to promote a positive outlook. For years people believed Tom Cruise to be taller than he was. It had nothing to do with his actual physical bearing, but rather from his presence in a room. At a shorter-than-average five foot six, he still managed to command the attention of everyone around him long before he became the multimillionaire star he is today.

Athletes are another example of this mind-over-matter attitude, especially marathon runners. Can you imagine the kind of mental strength it takes to push your body 26.2 miles at a run? I can barely imagine going ten miles on a bike or roller blades, but actually *running* that far! Yet thousands of people do it every year. They train every day, pushing themselves just that little bit farther, inch by inch, minute by minute, until one day they've run three hours without stopping once and are so far from home they need to call a cab to get back. Why? For no other reason than because they want to. It's a goal, a target, an ambition for them to reach the finish line. It's how they've chosen to invest time, and it's immensely satisfying.

I don't think the body was meant for that kind of torture! Mine isn't, at least. But strangely, for those who are willing to make the effort, their bodies become more than capable. Their muscles and bones become attuned to the pounding that takes place day after day. Some runners even say they feel lost without the exercise! To me, the life of a marathoner shows the power of strong convictions, determination, and positive thoughts to overcome setbacks, pain, challenge, and even physical limitations. Wouldn't it be nice to realize one day that your mind and body are "conditioned" for success? You can reach that point by deliberately making constructive changes on the training ground of your mind!

Think of most successful people you know, and you may agree that most are passionate about what they do, are rarely affected by negativity, and tend to enjoy their work. The better your attitude, the better your work and your life will be for you. If you know where you're going and you really want to get there, the only thing that can stop you is yourself.

Maybe your hope has been drowned out by loud and annoying negative monologues. But inside, aren't you desperate to believe that you're valued and unique with the potential to do great things? Well, go ahead and believe it, because it's true! Instead of playing the same game that has been defeating you for years, start taking your thoughts captive and decide you're going to play on the positive side of life for a while.

I'm not talking about becoming one of those braggarts who goes around constantly telling anyone and everyone how great he or she is. I'm talking about believing in your mission, knowing you're capable, and knowing you can excel.

I had the honor on television of interviewing Peggy Klaus, author of the book *Brag!: The Art of Tooting Your Own Horn without Blowing It*. She says there's nothing wrong with acknowledging your own potential. She even suggests preparing positive stories about yourself to be used at a moment's notice—tactfully, of course. This is something women struggle with. Maybe no one wants to hear it but you, and that's okay. The only one who *has* to hear it is you—every time you ask yourself if you can do it, every time you step up to take a chance, every time you hit a rough patch in your life, you need to hear just how strong, talented, and proficient you are in God. This is how you not only survive life, but how you exceed your expectations! This is how you outrun a lesser version of yourself.

ACTION APPLICATION
10 Questions to Test Your Thoughts and Words

Begin taking every thought and word captive by asking this question:

> Is this particular thought empowering or disempowering
> my investment of time?

These ten questions will help get you started:

1. What do I love most about my life and myself?

2. What am I most grateful for?

3. What thoughts do I have about myself that are holding me back?

ACTION APPLICATION

4. What words do I routinely use that are holding me back?

5. How am I letting these thoughts derail my success?

6. How am I letting my words derail my success?

7. How can I make my words work for me?

8. How can I replace these negative attitudes with life-affirming, God-inspired beliefs?

9. How can I turn these new, positive thoughts into actions?

10. What one thing can I do today to outrun a lesser version of myself?

PART THREE

Investing Time and Talents

7

Time for Your Loved Ones

This is how much God loved the world: He gave his Son, his one and only Son. And this is why: so that no one need be destroyed; by believing in him, anyone can have a whole and lasting life. God didn't go to all the trouble of sending his Son merely to point an accusing finger, telling the world how bad it was. He came to help, to put the world right again.

—JOHN 3:16–17 MSG

At the end of the day it's all about relationships, isn't it? With regard to time, the Bible consistently helps us focus on two things that matter most—our relationship with God and our relationships with people. That's not so easy for a project-focused, task-oriented person to wrap my mind around. But I know I've lost a great deal of time worrying about things that won't really matter at the end of the day.

Listen to these words of Jesus:

If God gives such attention to the appearance of wildflowers—most of which are never even seen—don't you think he'll attend to you, take pride in you, do his best for you? What I'm trying to do here is to get you to relax, not to be so preoccupied with *getting,* so you can respond to God's *giving.* People who don't know God and the way he works fuss over these things, but you know both God and how he works. Steep your life in God-reality, God-initiative, God-provisions. Don't worry about missing out. You'll find all your everyday human concerns will be met. (Matthew 6:30–33 MSG)

For the most balanced life, our investment of time in relationships should be first in God and then in others. But that's not so easy when the majority of Pressured women say people are the biggest obstacle to time management. One woman wrote, "OTHERS EXPECT TOO MUCH FROM ME AND TAKE ADVANTAGE OF ME AND MY TIME" (her caps, not mine). Another woman wrote, "I may be in the full swing of things and someone calls. I don't want to be rude, so sometimes I just say 'come on over' even though I have a lot going on at home."

More Connections, Fewer Relationships

Author Anthony Robbins sums it up nicely in saying, "The quality of your life is the quality of your relationships."[1] Let me take some liberties with that quote and change it to this statement: *The quality of your time is the quality of your relationships.* Our survey respondents get this. It's not surprising that women value time invested in caring for loved ones above all else.

Unfortunately, relationships seem to be in a crisis state in America. The way we relate to people is changing. Due to people's busy, hectic lives, "down time," when relationships can be formed and nurtured, has all but disappeared. Plus the advent of technology has made direct communications (in person or even via the telephone) a thing of the past. A good face-to-face chat is rare.

"Americans are far more socially isolated today than they were two decades ago," reads the first line of a recent article in the *Washington Post*. Addressing the concern of increased loneliness and isolation, reporter Shankar Vedantam found that a quarter of Americans say they have no one with whom they can discuss personal troubles, more than double the percent who felt similarly isolated in 1985. Overall, the number of people Americans have in their closest circle of confidants has dropped from around three to about two. Vedantam concludes, "If close social relationships support people in the same way that beams hold up buildings, more and more Americans appear to be dependent on a single beam."[2]

Studies show that people no longer count on their neighbors to the degree they used to (this number dropped by more than half from 19 percent to 8 percent) and that true friends are a rare find. Be honest; can you name the people who live next door or down the block? I'm guilty too.

So what exactly is going wrong with our investment in relationships and our lack of connection? Some findings show the separation to be a result of greater commute times and increased amounts of good ol' TV time, like these women who wrote us: "I spend too much time online or watching TV, even while working," and "Too much time spent walking to the bus stop, waiting for the bus, being at work, waiting for a bus, and walking home again."

Robert D. Putnam, professor of public policy at Harvard and the author of *Bowling Alone*, a book about the mounting social isolation within the United States, agreed with the findings of the study and said that they support the sentiments he has been expressing for years to skeptical audiences. "For most of the 20th century, Americans were becoming more connected with family and friends, and there was more giving of blood and money, and all of those trend lines turn sharply in the middle '60s and have gone in the other direction ever since," wrote Putnam. "[Today], Americans go on 60 percent fewer picnics and families eat dinner together 40 percent less often as compared with 1965. They are less likely to meet at clubs or go bowling in groups," continued Putnam.[3] So much for bowling night.

Of course, not everyone agrees with this study. In fact, University of Toronto sociologist Barry Wellman believes that people's overall ties were, in fact, growing during those same years. As compared with previous decades, this growth was due, in large part, to the internet. According to Wellman's calculations, within our contemporary society the average person has about 250 connections with friends and relatives. Wellman says, "My guess is people only have so much energy, and right now they are switching around a number of networks. . . . We are getting a division of labor in relationships. Some people give emotional aid, some people give financial aid."

Regardless of whether Putnam or Wellman is right, the fact is our society is changing—both in terms of our time priorities and the ways in which we connect with others. We may have more connections (and time interruptions), but are we really connecting in meaningful ways? Without picnics and neighborhood block parties, we may find ourselves relying more upon the internet in terms of fulfilling our relationship needs. Frightening thought.

Why Solid Relationships Matter

Forget the numerous emails and text messages you get throughout the day. Forget all the interruptions and requests for your time from acquaintances. Forget the huge number of names we keep in our databases of people we hardly know. Studies show that for solid, meaningful, deep relationships to develop, time well spent makes all the difference.

Older people who maintain social contacts, whether with a spouse or friends or through outside interests, are reported to have fewer medical problems. And older people who are married or who live with a roommate tend to be in better health than those who live alone.[4]

Take it from our former first lady Barbara Bush, who once said, "Cherish your human connections—your relationships with friends and family."[5] Relationships enrich a person's life in ways that no material, monetary, or accomplishment gain can. They add warmth, caring, support and nurturing, companionship, stress reduction— the list is virtually endless. When my husband and I were experiencing the pain of two lost babies, I can't tell you how much my friends at church and in the workplace meant to me. There are times in life when you just feel numb in the confusion of your circumstances. I'll always be grateful for the empathetic souls God has placed in our lives. Really, nourishment of the soul begins with the building of quality relationships, including a personal relationship with God.

Fewer Relationships, Solid Connections

Volumes have been written on managing and maintaining our relationships, but I'm looking at this investment of your days simply in terms of time. By that standard, nobody was a better investor of his time than Jesus. So what can we learn from the Master of time?

Jesus invested his life and ministry primarily in twelve men. That's it. Yes, he spoke to the crowds. Yes, he healed the multitudes. Yes, he even invested a few choice words to put the religious leaders of the day in their place. But he didn't write a book or hire a publicist to get his message out. His life-altering, world-changing strategy was investing time in a small group of committed friends. Lowly, unpretentious friends. These weren't the rich and powerful of society. Chances are none of the guys Jesus hung out with would make the "dream team" on a Fortune 500 company list. Fishermen? A tax gatherer (not so popular in that day either!)?

But in this little ragtag group, Jesus saw a few committed friends who would go on to change the world. He saw the best in them. And he still sees the best in every one of us. He staked his time and impact on relationships—then and now. He loves people no matter what they will or won't give in return. He loved to the point of death and never wasted one moment of time putting conditions on that love, even for the one friend who betrayed him. For me, it's hard to completely understand this type of love, especially during times that I feel so unlovable. I guess intellectually I'll never comprehend why or how the Lord loves us so entirely, sacrificially. But I have learned to accept it by faith. And there are moments when I truly sense his overpowering love, like the benevolent love of a father for his children. This is why it really has become such a joy to follow him, knowing that I've put my heart and my life in the hands of the one who is compassionate and patient toward me and always knows the right path for me to take.

The apostle Paul also tells us to follow in the footsteps of Jesus in letting our thoughts dwell on the good in people, not everything they do wrong: "Summing it all up, friends, I'd say you'll do best by filling your minds and meditating on things true, noble, reputable, authentic, compelling, gracious—the best, not the worst; the beautiful, not the ugly; things to praise, not things to curse" (Philippians 4:8 MSG).

What we see in others, we bring out in them. If we focus on someone else's negative points to the point of even criticizing them, you can be certain the negativity will only increase. However, if we choose to focus on the good in someone and praise them for these attributes, this act of kindness brings out the best in them and in us as well. The better we feel about them, the less we feel the need to nag, criticize, or complain—wasting their time and ours. When is the last time you called a friend just to give a kind word of encouragement? Can you think of a better use of time?

Limit Access to Yourself

This is especially for all you Overwhelmed, Pressured, and Self-Stressed ladies. We feel guilty if we're not available for everyone at all times. "Constant interruptions" were top on the list of our survey's time stealers. Think about it. We don't allow ourselves any real private time anymore. No longer can we escape to the grocery store without the kids calling on the cell phone to tell us the dog got sprayed by a skunk. Sure, if you didn't have the cell phone, you'd be surprised when you got home. But now when you get the call, you feel the urge to rush your shopping and get home to take care of the mess. The stress builds, and you get home only to realize that you forgot half the items on your list. That really wasn't good time management. It was stress overload.

Simple Strategies to Limit Access to Yourself

▶ **Become well acquainted with the Off button on your cell phone.**

▶ **Let voice mail take messages on your home or office phone.**

▶ **If you have a door at your home or workplace office, use it.**

▶ **Practice using the word *no*.**

▶ **Learn to recognize those who are needlessly sapping your time and set firm boundaries.**

And it's not just our families and friends who have unlimited access to our personal time. We make ourselves available for our bosses and clients at any time, night or day. It just seems like good business practice, doesn't it? No way. Reality check: it's pressure on top of more pressure. Thanks to technology, we can be reached day or night, whether we're on vacation, at the doctor's office, or out to eat with our families. But do we really need to be that accessible? Even Jesus took time to retreat from the crowds to recharge his spiritual batteries. Sometimes you just have to be alone if you're going to get anything done.

Limiting our accessibility is tough. It took me a long time before I gave myself permission even to shut the door to my office at work. I had to realize that being a nice and helpful person didn't mean letting everyone walk into my work space at any moment to talk about anything. Let's face it—uninvited visitors or callers can steal your time away in a flash! Don't be rude, but try to end the conversation or visit politely.

Of course, this is where we have to be sensitive to the leading of the Holy Spirit. If someone's truly in need, there's no more valuable use of your time. But if your fellow worker or neighbor is bored and just feels like killing time in your space, perhaps you can find a way to gently nudge the person toward the soon-to-be softly closing door.

We need to keep this principle in mind for our personal lives too. How many times have you found yourself at meetings or functions that really don't have anything to do with you? Instead of excusing yourself, you waste time by sitting through the entire ordeal because, well, you want to maintain that "nice" image. You don't want to seem rude. Next time, politely find the nearest exit and run, not walk, toward it!

Before we assume that others are always to blame, we need to examine our own time-wasting tactics toward others. How many times have we been late for an appointment and wasted someone else's time? How many times have we burst into someone's office to chat, without asking if this was a good time for her? We have to remember to be considerate and thoughtful, not only of our time, but of others' as well. I admit, even as I'm writing this, I can think of many times I sat down in someone's office, with a great story to tell, without asking them, "Hey, do you have the time?"

Two-Faced Technology

Just like so many things in life, technology in and of itself isn't bad—it's how we use and manage it that determines whether it will be helpful or harmful. What did our grandparents do without cell phones? They ate nice meals with their families, shared quality time with their children on vacation, and read a five-month-old magazine in the doctor's office. They wrote letters, long ones. And when people came to stay with them, our grandparents were there to host, to be present with their precious friends or family.

But now sales people tell us that technology helps us gain time, stay connected, and become more productive, but it's not hard to see that all these gadgets and chips can work either for or against us. In terms of time-wasting interruptions, technology can be your best friend or your worst enemy. I would probably be lost without my computer and Palm scheduler, and I'm a huge fan of caller ID. However, despite all the high-tech hype, we still don't seem to have enough time in our days to do what needs to be done. Plus, if we let them, many of these tools can end up robbing us of our precious personal time, which adds to our sense of being overwhelmed.

You may want to consider the unthinkable. After all, your cell phone, pager, PDA, BlackBerry, and other communication devices actually have an On/Off switch. And it works! Try turning it to Off for a few moments each day while you're trying to focus on something of your choice or just some much-needed downtime. Silence can truly be golden. If you would never think of turning your cell phone all the way off, how about letting your voice mail take your calls and returning messages only twice a day? (Family calls don't count, of course. Unless the dog got sprayed by a skunk—Daddy can handle that!)

Managing technology begins with knowing that you have that ability instead of letting technology manage you. For example, learning to use your DVR can cut your "must-see TV" time in half, when you lose the commercials and watch what you truly want to watch, rather than "filler TV" while you wait for a program to come on or see if it's a new episode. How about reading emails only at the beginning of the day and in the afternoon? A good spam filter will also help you weed out useless correspondence, if you can call it that. Pop-up blockers will no longer alert you that you've just "Won a new car! Simply click here." You can develop your own strategies for managing technology and interruptions in your schedule. You have the right to say no here as well.

Creative Ways to Say No

Speaking of the word *no*, there are times when you Pressured ladies have to use it. If you don't, you're quickly going to join our Overwhelmed, with all the things you've agreed to do! Still, many women have a problem using this word. In truth, most people don't like to say no; we feel better when we can agree. But there's a price to pay for the times when saying yes is the equivalent of giving in. Give in too much, and you'll find yourself overworked, overextended, and burned out.

You can get over the guilt of delivering a rejection by just qualifying your response. Here are a few options for turning someone down graciously, without enduring a pang of guilt.

Not now. Let's say you're asked to help with a fundraiser at your child's school. You feel terrible turning down this nice person who wants your help, but you're already stressed with numerous tasks. Guess what? You can get out of it without appearing to be disinterested. Try this: "I would love to help out because this is a great cause, and the school is so important to our family. My time is so limited right now, but if you can give me a little more advance notice, I'd be happy to consider helping next time."

Or let's say a coworker asks you to help out by taking on her duties. You feel like she's just being lazy or simply doesn't want to do what she should. Helping out this time will most likely mean she'll identify you as an easy mark. You'll then get requests to help her again and again, piling more work onto your already-burdened shoulders. So tell her that you've got a full list of tasks of your own and can't help right now. Ask if it can wait until next week or some other time in the future. You haven't said no, but only "not now." Most likely, she'll trot off and look for another unsuspecting victim, and you have the satisfaction of having delivered a guilt-free rejection.

Not quite. You can also diffuse the bad feeling of turning down a polite request by offering a "not quite" instead. When asked if you can take on coaching duties for your child's soccer team, try: "I'm going to be tied up that day, but can I provide drinks or snacks for the kids? I can drop them off at school on my way to work." When you offer a compromise, it can be just as good as a yes.

Not me. Perhaps you just can't help out by giving of your own time, but you know someone else who might be a great alternative. Sometimes offering a referral is a positive option. By doing so, you have, in fact, offered assistance.

Don't confuse saying no with being negative. You have to set boundaries once in a while. Sometimes the good feeling you get from being agreeable comes at the price of lost time and your own well-being.

The Negative Purge

Jesse and Sheila work as a team at an advertising agency. Jesse develops the ideas, and Sheila presents them to the client. But first, Sheila brings a project to Jesse—outlining the goals, the client's product, and the parameters, which include budget, schedule, and specifications such as the size of an ad or a brochure.

Sheila says that almost every time she holds this initial meeting, Jesse gives her a litany of reasons why it won't work. The idea isn't enterprising or creative. The budget's too tight. The schedule's unrealistic. There's no way it's going to happen according to Sheila's plans, and she's just going to have to tell her client to live with it.

Sheila used to go into panic mode because of Jesse's negativism. She would immediately begin phrasing the presentation to her client in terms of getting more time, increasing the budget, selling a different idea, or otherwise accommodating the obstacles Jesse just tossed in her path. She was overcome with anxiety, worried about getting what she needed to keep the client happy.

On each project, however, there came a point when suddenly everything changed. Jesse would come through. In fact, the more Jesse stressed over an assignment, the better the outcome.

Once Sheila caught on, she learned not to internalize Jesse's initial negativity but instead turn it into a positive. She let Jesse fume about a client's unrealistic expectations and the harried schedule.

She listened wordlessly while Jesse ranted about the lack of creativity and how clients just didn't understand what works and why. Ultimately, Sheila would punctuate the tantrums with a positive statement: "Okay, Jesse. I totally understand your concerns, but I know you're a talented designer and a consummate professional. See what you can do with what I'm giving you. I've got complete faith in your abilities and whatever you come up with will be appreciated."

You have to stand for something or you'll fall for anything.

In less than ten seconds Sheila gave Jesse praise, encouragement, support, and appreciation, instead of quickly following her earlier inclinations to advise Jesse to "Shut up and do what you're paid to do!"

Sheila came to refer to Jesse's diatribes as a negative purge, releasing all the junk from her system in order to think creatively. Once Jesse had sputtered for a little while, she was "cleansed." Then Jesse could settle down and go to work without pent-up frustration.

The key for Sheila was not to waste time by falling prey to this negative pattern and to just understand this was how her partner communicated. Understanding Jesse's unique personality and needs became a better time investment for both of them.

Your Values, Your Time

You've certainly heard the expression that you "have to stand for something or you'll fall for anything." Pressured and Self-Stressed ladies, this may ring true for you—if you act wishy-washy and let other people always exert dominance and walk all over you.

Jesus was never wishy-washy. He was never swayed by the negativity or even the good intentions of true friends. When his devoted follower Peter tried to dissuade him from his destiny in going to the cross, Jesus put him in his place. When political leaders tried to use him to advance their goals, he made it clear that he was interested in advancing another kingdom.

Of course, sticking to your values means clearly knowing what it is you stand for. Likewise, others won't know who you really are if you're continually pretzel-bending yourself to accommodate others' needs and wishes.

In our survey, some of the Pressured women wrote that what prevented them from better time management was "doing things for everyone else," "too many demands for one person," "no help when I need it—kids needing this or that—or a helpless man needing me to do everything for him." While your intentions may be good and your objective may be to have people like you (this is called being a "people pleaser"), what tends to happen is that others lose respect for you and also often take advantage of you. More time wasted.

Believe me, I understand! But before you can take charge of your time, you have to realize that this is within your power to change. Others won't change, but you can. As you begin to teach people how to respect your time—and that this principle is nonnegotiable—the results will be amazing, and you'll feel freer than ever.

In respecting others' time, it's important to note that Jesus also never wasted his time trying to control others or pushing his values on them. He stated his point, then moved on. A true gentleman. Case in point: when asked by a rich man how he could ensure entry into the kingdom of heaven, Jesus gave him a three-step plan; "Sell everything you have and give to the poor, and you will have treasure in heaven. Then come, follow me" (Mark 10:21 NIV).

Easy, right? Not really. And the rich man walked away disheartened.

You see, Jesus knew where the man's true priorities were and didn't go running after him or beat him over the head, saying, "Do you know who you're talking to? I have plans for you that would blow away your measly dreams!" Jesus simply let the man walk away.

How often have we wasted time by trying to fix or change another person? An honest relationship involves accepting the person for exactly who and what he is. For example, when you first met the person, he told you he had no interest in getting married and settling down—why now, just because you've invested two years in this relationship, do you think you can get this person to do otherwise? Your thought may be that if he really likes and cares about you, he will do this one thing for you. Yet changing his ways is not a part of the original deal. Rather, the up-front agreement was that you both liked and accepted each other exactly as you were.

So as not to just beat up on Mixed Emotions, who hasn't wasted time trying to change or fix someone who really doesn't want to change? I know I've done this with friendships. I'll never forget spending an entire day with a dear friend as she talked about how badly her husband was treating her and that she didn't know what to do. Together we came up with a plan for her to get help, find a support group, and set some firm boundaries. The next day she came to me wanting to talk about how badly her husband was treating her and that she didn't know what to do. I felt like I was in the movie, *Groundhog Day* with Bill Murray—the story of a weatherman who keeps waking up to repeat Groundhog Day, over and over again. In talking with my friend, even the sentences we were saying were the same as the previous day's. It was then I realized that she didn't really want to change anything; she just wanted to talk about it. And talk about it. And talk about it.

It's an incredible waste of time to try to exert control over another person who really doesn't want to change. Only God can change the heart of another person. We can pray. We can encourage, but we only waste time when we try to step into God's role.

Relationship Time Check

In taking a good look at time and your friendships, here are a few thoughts to consider:

▶ *Motivation check.* Be honest with yourself in asking why you're interested in the other person. Does she inspire you to be a better person? When you can answer that question, you can determine whether you sincerely want to build this relationship.

▶ *Give it time.* If you aren't sure you want to form a relationship with a particular person, take it slow as acquaintances. The two of you might speak on occasion, and given time, should you find the person to be interesting and trustworthy (and vice versa), you may want to invest in building a more solid connection.

▶ *Judge not . . .* Do your best not to exercise any preconceived notions or harsh criticisms about someone until you actually get to know the person. If you immediately make snap judgments about people and turn them away, you may be missing out on people whose company you may actually enjoy.

> ▸*Listen to your instinct*—and that of the Holy Spirit tell-
> ing you this may not be the best relationship for you.
> Every lady I've met—me included—has made the mis-
> take of giving her time to someone she knows is not the
> best for her. Sometimes, despite our very best inten-
> tions, we can end up in relationships with people who,
> once we get to know them, are not who they initially ap-
> peared to be. Some master manipulators are very good at
> keeping their tricky ways under wraps until they're con-
> vinced you're 100 percent under their rapturous spell.

The easiest way to spot a master manipulator or false friend is to listen to her words and watch her actions. Do the two add up? Jesus said we will know people by "their fruits"—by what they produce in their lives. Seeing that takes time.

Also, before blindly stepping into a relationship, note these three things:

Is he coercive? Is he always trying to get you do things his way? Is "his" way better than yours? After being around this person awhile, you may even begin to doubt yourself.

Will the relationship be time-intensive? Does this person seem to be overly needy, always demanding your attention and time? This can leave you feeling extremely depleted and resentful of having to invest so much of yourself in the relationship.

Is she overly competitive? Is everything a big competition? Who has the most money? Who has the most friends? Who has the better job or more interesting volunteer position? If this friendship leaves you feeling inadequate or diminished, you may want to reconsider.

Really listen to what people say about themselves. Usually, in time, they'll tell you exactly who they are and why they're interested in you.

Room to Grow

While Jesus clearly set limits, he also gave grace and mercy. That's what he's all about. Nobody is perfect, and that's why we so desperately need him. He's also the God of second chances, and this is the perspective we can also have in connecting with others. In looking at ourselves, relationships are the tool God uses to teach a certain lesson. From each other, we learn to grow, change, and mature. Yet when you each begin to change, it may be in slightly different ways. It's important then to acknowledge this and, at times, let the person go,[6] or at the very least, grow.

While the people in our lives may come and go, there's one relationship that will never fail. Jesus will always let you grow and never let you go. He says he will never leave you or forsake you. Even on the days that I feel most alone, this is one thing I'm absolutely sure of. When he says his love for you is eternal, unshakeable, unconditional, you can trust that.

Today's women certainly have their fair share of issues with which to contend. From the work world to the home life, there's an endless array of people whose needs are just waiting to be met. Just remember, as you dive into your busy schedule filled with emails, voice mails, and other interruptions, there's Someone who quietly, consistently waits for you to invest time in the most solid connection available. Jesus is and always will be your best investment of time. By investing in him, you'll find yourself.

Invest Yourself Where It Matters

1. Say hello to someone at work/school/church whom you've never spoken with before.

2. Learn someone's name and use it when greeting them. (This is for me! I'm terrible at remembering names.)

3. Learn the names of your next-door neighbors and deliver chocolate chip cookies (my favorite!).

4. Take one minute for one act of random kindness to the person you like least. Oooh, this is hard, but surely we can send an encouraging card?

5. If you have children, have them also repeat steps 1–4 above. (If your neighbors aren't home, they can send the chocolate-chip cookies my way.)

ACTION APPLICATION

Testing Your Relationships

Have you ever really evaluated your relationships in terms of time invested?

Ask yourself these questions:

1. What would Jesus do in this relationship?

2. Would he invest in this person, or would he simply let her or him walk away?

3. How much time is this person taking from my schedule?

4. Is this time that I enjoy giving?

5. If I could invest in a relationship with anyone, who would it be and why?

Time for Work
That Matters

We are His workmanship, created in Christ Jesus for good works, which
God prepared beforehand so that we would walk in them.

—EPHESIANS 2:10 NASB

There are moments in our work when we feel unappreciated, overwhelmed, stressed out, and downright miserable. That's normal whether you work at home or in an office. But what happens when you feel like that all the time? When every day you wake up and dread the day ahead of you? What do you do when you know you have to make a career change but you're just not sure what it is you want to be doing? Where do you even begin?

Believe me, I've been there. I've been in jobs where each day felt like a literal nightmare. They had me pulling the sheets over my head as the morning alarm screamed that it was time to get up and get ready for another day of pain and suffering. I know more than my fair share of women who took "temporary" jobs until they could find their dream job, but guess what? They got trapped, and before they knew it, they'd spent ten years of their lives in a doomed, dead-end job. What happened? I spent way too much time reporting bad news when I really wanted to tell people the good news of Christ.

So many of us ask ourselves every day, *Where did the time go? What happened to my dream of* [fill in the blank]? Where did we take the wrong turn? How did we end up here after making all those big plans?

The money does it every time. You might be the single mother who believes she can't afford to look for another job. Or the wife of someone who recently lost his job due to downsizing. Or the single woman who enjoys the life of luxury (i.e., shoes) over a fulfilling career that may mean less money.

Another reason we tend to stay in going-nowhere jobs is that we crave security. We want to know what will happen tomorrow. We like security, whether it's in relationships or careers. And security means pay, health benefits, and yes, even routines. We get stuck deeply in routines, especially if we have children. Routine equals security? Not really. Venturing out into the unknown is a rare quality, and if you're a woman who seeks risks and scoffs at the idea of schedules and routines, I applaud you (although you probably wouldn't be reading this, because you'd just be too busy taking a risk without a care in the world).

And then there's fear. Fear of the unknown. Fear of what the future will hold. Fear of failure. So we stay put, firm in our cubicles, and convince ourselves we just can't do it.

Oh, and the excuses we can come up with! Like "I'm too old"; "I'm too young"; "It's not my choice"; "I don't have what it takes"; "I'm overqualified"; "It's familiar and comfortable here."

But here's a news flash: no job will ever give you complete security. No position will ever completely fulfill you. Ultimately, true fulfillment will come only through our relationship with Christ. However, for many women, the time they invest in their work lives is a huge chunk of the time they spend on this earth. Before you make any more excuses of why you can't follow your dream and find the career that's right for you, think again. There *are* ways. There *are* options. There may be failures and frustrations, but in the long run, you'll be relieved that you stepped out of your comfort zone and ventured into the unknown.

So what keeps us from investing our time in truly satisfying work?

I Can't Take It Anymore!

Consider Jodi. As a child, she was an avid reader and grew up thinking she could be anything she wanted to be. While earning Cs in algebra and chemistry, she was always one of the strongest students in her English classes.

In her senior year, Jodi decided to attend a local college and major in English. However, once she graduated, she was racked with anxiety because everyone kept asking what she would do with her degree. Friends and family joked that she could look forward to flipping burgers. After taking a series of dead-end temp jobs, she decided to go to law school, since everyone kept telling her that was her best choice for success. She figured that since she liked to read and could comprehend written materials quickly and didn't mind spending time at the library working on research papers, she already had the basic talent required to be a lawyer.

Jodi finished law school because she didn't want to be seen as a quitter and needed to find a career. She didn't want to let everyone down. Besides, she thought, being successful was more important than being happy, right?

However, she soon discovered that a fondness for reading didn't mean she would like being an attorney. Plodding daily in her chosen career, Jodi resented the long hours that junior associates were expected to log at her law firm. In the end, she had no time to read anything other than legal briefs. To make matters worse, she worried constantly about the amount of student-loan debt she carried from law school, so she decided to switch to corporate law in the hope that she could make more money and get her debt paid off. It would just be for a few years, right? As practical as that may seem, her plan committed her to spending a considerable amount of time at a job that didn't suit her talents and, worse, made her unhappy.

Jodi learned, at the high cost of precious time, that what you like doesn't necessarily match up with something you're passionate about. After some soul-searching, she took a position as an editorial assistant at a publishing house. I'd love to report that she finally found her true passion (she didn't), but she found her new position more satisfying than practicing law. Also, having alleviated a major source of stress in her life (her job), she's better able to focus more clearly on finding and applying her true talents. Like many women, Jodi is slowly coming to a point where she's even happier living with fewer material things and more time to herself. As her work life is beginning to gradually improve, making choices such as taking in a roommate to lower the rent payment and pay off her debts doesn't seem so bad.

Like many of us, Jodi is still searching for her true calling.

Find Your Buried Talents

Then there's a common misconception that the road to a lasting sense of purpose—in both work and life—will one day magically appear before you. The stories often go something like this: A child receives a toy stethoscope for Christmas, kindling an unwavering lifelong desire to practice medicine. Or a stay-at-home mom whose baked goods are so extraordinarily delicious finally realizes that she is meant to go into business for herself. Or a teen lands a slot on *American Idol,* launching her dream of becoming a multiplatinum recording artist.

Yet while few are fortunate enough to find their true talents through a combination of innate ability or happenstance, the rest of us struggle to hear even the faintest whisper of our "true calling." How do you know what your true, innate, God-given talents are?

In order to find our real purpose in life—the area in which we should be investing our time—we need to listen for the strong whisper in our hearts. But this process of self-discovery is often fraught with uncertainty when the regular demands of our everyday lives seem so pressing. We ask how we'll find the time to "discover ourselves" while earning a living and tending to the needs of those who depend on us. It's no wonder we backburner our desire for connection and purpose. If we don't, who will clean the house, pay the mortgage, and make the car payment?

We also begin to worry that the search for our true talents is inherently selfish, convincing ourselves that it may require a career change, plunging us deep into financial and emotional turmoil. For many of us, this is enough to keep us stuck in jobs or relationships that don't suit us while working hard to maintain lifestyles that don't speak to our needs. This isn't to say these fears are unreasonable, but one of the first steps in finding a deeper sense of meaning is developing the willingness to look at your fears and understand that pushing them aside will prevent you from leading the most fulfilling life possible.

From our survey, it's clear that many Procrastinators put off doing something because they simply don't know what to do. One woman wrote that she let other people tell her how things should be done. Others said their biggest time challenge is their "mental attitude" or "lack of initiative or ambition." These worries are not proof of an immature or irresponsible person. They may, in fact, demonstrate a real caring and concern for the people and things most important to them, and they may contain the raw material that will help them determine their true paths. The fact is, we stay in relationships, jobs, and places that don't suit us for a number of reasons, most of which are related to fear.

I mentioned earlier the story Jesus told that we call the parable of the talents. He used this parable to illustrate our financial responsibilities. Let's look at it more closely. It begins with a man who was going on a trip. Before he did, he left his servants money (also referred to as "talents") to invest. He gave one servant five talents, another two talents, and the last servant one talent. He went away, and the servants went to work—or at least two of them did, taking risks and doubling their money and receiving a reward and praise from their boss when he got back home. As we talked about earlier in the book, the last servant was afraid and buried his talent in the sand.

Do you understand his motivations? I do. Let's read about this last guy as the moment came to face the big guy:

He said, "Sir, I know that you are a hard man. You gather grain where you have not planted. You take up where you have not spread out. I was afraid and I hid your money in the ground.

191

See! Here is your money." His owner said to him, "You bad and lazy servant. You knew that I gather grain where I have not planted. You knew that I take up where I have not spread out. You should have taken my money to the bank. When I came back, I could have had my own money and what the bank paid for using it. Take the one piece of money from him. Give it to the one who has ten pieces of money. "For the man who has will have more given to him. He will have more than enough. The man who has nothing, even what he has will be taken away. (Matthew 25:24–29 NLV)

Talk about a tough life lesson! But it's also a lesson in reality. God watches and hopes we'll multiply and become good stewards of our money and our literal talents! But how many of us are more like the last man, who buried the piece of silver and his true gifts from God in the ground?

Our true talents are linked not only to our passions but to our sense of purpose. This link is so important that many psychologists have sought to quantify how central it is to our health and sense of well being. For example, in a 2003 UCLA survey of nearly four thousand undergraduates from across the United States, 86 percent of respondents identified "attaining wisdom" as a major life goal, in addition to becoming a more loving and compassionate person (84 percent), seeking beauty in their lives (67 percent), attaining a sense of inner harmony (60 percent), developing a meaningful life philosophy (52 percent), becoming a better person (30 percent), and searching for purpose in life (75 percent).[1] Also, psychologist C. D. Ryff observed that, among the six dimensions of psychological well-being she identified, one of the most important was finding purpose in life. This was considered a major determinant of positive mental health.[2]

So how do we go about understanding this purpose for our lives—plus our true talents and how to invest them? According to the Bible, we can gain wisdom by simply *asking:*

First, *ask God.* Just as God will multiply your time, he will also increase your wisdom in how to invest the talents he's given you. After all, he came up with his plan for you, and he promises to give you whatever you lack in wisdom to carry it out: "If any of you lacks wisdom, he should ask God, who gives generously to all without finding fault, and it will be given to him" (James 1:5–6 NIV).

Next, *ask yourself.* Here are three questions to consider:

1. What do I love?

2. What am I good at doing?

3. What energizes me?

4. What are my weaknesses?

Finally, *ask others* (cautiously). This is another effective way to determine our core strengths—directly enlisting those around us by asking a few simple questions. Make a list of friends and family whose opinion you value and get their feedback. Don't feel inhibited because you think you'll seem like you're fishing for compliments. Start by explaining that you're thinking about the next phase of your work life and that you highly value their input. Explain that you need their help in determining what your strengths are, because you want to explore your options.

In some cases, there may be people (even those closest to you) who don't understand and who will either deliberately or inadvertently discourage you. They'll ask what's wrong with your current job and tell you to stop worrying because, after all, no one really likes her work.

Here are examples of the questions you can ask others: "Can you describe a time that I was especially helpful to you?" "What was I doing when I seemed happiest to you?" "What kind of work can you see me doing?" (I'm not talking about just working for money; this can also be philanthropy in your community or volunteering in your church. These folks are some of the hardest workers I know!)

Also ask them to use three adjectives that best describe you. Writer and acting coach Corey Blake uses this exercise to help actors identify their strengths so they (and, ideally, casting directors) will choose the roles that best suit them and that will be most readily acceptable and believable to audiences.[3]

Although you might not necessarily have all the answers at the end of the exercise, you do stand a good chance of learning something about yourself.

Author Po Bronson gives us a different perspective: "Most of us don't get epiphanies." We get only a whisper—a faint urge. That's it. That's the call. It's up to you to do the work of discovery, to connect it to an answer. Of course, there's never a single right answer. At some point, it feels right enough that you choose, and the energy formerly spent casting about is now devoted to making your choice fruitful.[4]

Others have called this "listening for the still, small voice of God." Usually God doesn't yell at you. He whispers.

Your Work Matters

So why should we ascribe so much importance to the role of work in the search for our true talents?

While work certainly isn't the end of the story, it often is the gateway to leading a well-rounded life, whether you work at home with children or in an office for a corporation. Certainly your vocation is only one factor in your investment of time, as we see from our survey. For some people, a job is nothing more than a means to an end—a way to support their passions *outside* of the office. If you find that you're able to do that, more power to you. If you discover that your happiness lies in not defining yourself by your work, then you've uncovered wisdom that will illuminate the way you structure the other aspects of your life. You'll no longer use your occupation as the measure of your happiness and success, leaving you more room and more time to explore God's unique plan for your life. After all, Jesus spent time working as a carpenter before he launched his ministry that would revolutionize the world.

Although Jodi received some bad career advice from friends and family, this isn't to say that getting outside input isn't important. In Jodi's case, others' advice and intentions led her to base one of her biggest decisions—her career—on *their* fears. It's natural for our loved ones to want to help, and one way they try is by offering unsolicited advice and suggestions. This can have a huge impact on you when you're anxious or unhappy and might ultimately encourage you to make poor choices. That's why the Bible teaches us to seek wise, not fearful, counsel.

Jodi's initial love of reading led her down a particular path, but finding the exact place that best suited her abilities has been much more difficult. By at least committing to the process of finding your life's work, you might be less likely to make a major commitment (such as earning a degree) on the basis of insecurity and confusion. You won't waste your weekends dreading Mondays.

The Test of Temperament

Everyone has a special gift, and once you know what it is, do it with passion. It's a God-given, unique talent to make your mark on the world. Some women are great analytical thinkers, while others are more artistic or creative. And then there are the fortunate few who have the combined left-brain and right-brain talents. Regardless of our individual gifting, we all have a deep desire burning inside of us that will send off warning signals to tell us we're not in the right place, with the right person, or even in the right job. Trust yourself! Trust God!

Human-resource professionals are fond of the phrase "goodness of fit." Goodness of fit goes beyond whether or not a potential employee has the skills, education, and training to perform a certain set of tasks. It also considers personality factors such as innate ability, leadership, team-building potential, attitude, and temperament in evaluating an employee's chances of not just performing, but excelling at a job. Since corporations now consider a constellation of factors in developing their employees' potential, one of the most popular and reliable assessment tools is the Myers-Briggs personality model that we earlier saw referred to in the Wikipedia article on decision making.

Personality-assessment tests have been around for nearly a century, and employers often use the Myers-Briggs model to help them determine effective training and development opportunities based on their employee's talents. This model is based on the theories of Swiss psychologist Carl Jung, who believed that with the right insight into the individual's emotional and cognitive world, you could predict certain aspects of human behavior. Jung's theories identified three personality preference scales and eight distinct personality types.

Intrigued by Jung's approach, two American women, Katherine Briggs and her daughter Isabel Briggs Myers began in the early twentieth century to develop a personality typing system to map the similarities and differences between different personalities. After years of study, Myers and Briggs eventually identified sixteen personality types and created a test instrument called the Myers-Briggs Type Indicator (MBTI) in the 1940s.

In previous decades, human resources had come under the influence of something called trait psychology, which viewed human nature as a combination of particular personality traits. In creating job descriptions, hiring managers used this model to discover which traits seemed best suited for each position and then to recruit employees with the closest match. However, the Myers-Briggs model went beyond that—providing a picture of a candidate's individual makeup, rather than relying on a set list of abstract skills and qualifications. It took into account how someone could be both detail-oriented and spontaneous, or a critical thinker who is also a team builder.

These tests can be useful because they help us uncover our weaknesses and strengths and what motivates and energizes us. They also help us determine which type of work environment is best suited to our personality preferences and not just our skills.

Case in point—my failed attempt at taking an engineering physics class during my freshman year of college. I was always pretty decent at math, and my father and I thought I could handle one of these classes. How hard could it be? Hey, I have one brother who's an engineer and another who has a doctorate in math. A doctorate! In math! It took me about a week to figure out that I didn't belong in that program (especially when I could barely understand the engineering language—they speak their own language, you know!), so I dropped that class as fast as I could. God bless my father who also thought I would love taking a geology class; after all, he's a geophysicist. Turns out the apple fell way far away from his family tree, because I barely passed that class. My father did give me good advice in getting a business degree, so for that, thanks Dad!

Understanding your personality type is a good start because it allows you to depersonalize the situation (and the accompanying sense of failure). More often than not, the issue refers to the question of "goodness of fit" as opposed to your individual skills and personality. This is especially important if you've been struggling with a job you don't like, when it's easy to assume it's all your fault. The truth is, no one really excels at things that don't interest them.

He Is the Visionary

Earlier I mentioned how meeting with the Lord in prayer and reading is the key to a successful, well-ordered day. This help also goes beyond just day-to-day tasks. If you ask him, he will also give you wisdom about your true calling that also goes far beyond any personality test. Sure, take those tests; it's a good beginning. But view the results with a grain of salt, because many times in life God will require you to do work that is way outside of your comfort zone. A job that scares you and is beyond your own skills and personality traits is a job that only he can empower you to accomplish. It's called learning. Growing. Outrunning lesser versions of yourself and assuming the role of manager of your time. While God, as our CEO, will give us power and wisdom to reinvent our lives, it's up to us to take action to actually change them.

In learning some of the technical aspects of my business, I'll never forget what author and speaker Tom Antion told me: "Carolyn, you are the visionary. You direct your business." He's written many books, including *The Ultimate Guide to Electronic Marketing for Small Business,* and he is a computer genius. Computers for me, on the other hand, are way outside of my comfort zone but something I've had to learn to manage. He told me that while I can certainly hire someone to take care of the daily challenges of technology, it was up to me to understand the process. In stepping up to the role of visionary, I've had to step out of my comfort zone on many occasions. I've had to throw any perceived personality traits and tests out the office window in order to get the job done.

Think for a moment. How has the Lord taken you out of your comfort zone to move you closer to your true calling?

Your Values, Your Vocation

So if tests won't give us the whole career picture, how can we discern whether or not we're investing our time in the right workplace? And, as many of us know, sometimes that workplace can be right at home.

Recently I had the opportunity to interview a number of highly successful network-marketing salespeople who shared their stories of finding jobs they love. All these people were six-figure earners who had won every sales award offered by their respective companies. I was struck by how similar their stories were and how many of their personal narratives seemed to overlap at crucial periods in their lives. Of the people I interviewed, almost half discovered their true calling only after undergoing major life stress, such as serious financial challenges, while the others were aware of certain preferences and personality factors and more or less stumbled upon their chosen fields by accident.

One of the women I interviewed is a top distributor for a health-products company. A single mother, she struggled to make ends meet and held a number of different jobs, ranging from high school teacher to antiques dealer. An acquaintance approached her about joining a network-marketing company. Looking for direction in her life, she decided to give it a try. For a few years she halfheartedly worked the business but didn't see significant results. However, she was introduced to a line of health-care products (the ones she sells today) and felt passionate about them from the start. She felt committed to spreading the word. Because she had a true passion for the products, she had no reservations about recommending them to friends. Further, now that she had the motivation to sell something she truly loved, she also began to believe more firmly in the network-marketing business model, which she described as "being in business for yourself, but not by yourself."

Her strong belief in the philosophy of her organization motivated her to succeed big-time. During our interview, I was amazed that she seemed to be so passionately engaged in her work. The company also emphasized personal development, and because she had been through so many struggles, the opportunity to work through her feelings and to give herself, in Zig Ziglar's words, a "check-up from the neck up" inspired her. She knew that in order to succeed in her business, she needed to outrun a lesser version of herself.

As we talked, she mentioned how gratifying it is to see new members of her down-line (the group of people she's recruited into her sales force) make their first commissions. One of the most satisfying aspects of her job was how it facilitated close relationships with her colleagues. She was energized by the training process and seemed to have a real personal interest and investment in their success.

If you're familiar with network marketing, you're probably thinking, *Well, of course she wanted her sales force to succeed because it bene-*

fits her. But the commission she earned on her recruits' sales had no effect on her whatsoever. She's made enough money now that she doesn't need to worry about it anymore. Yet she shared with other women the same ability to transcend the financial rewards of her career in order to have the freedom to focus on how she can be of service to others.

I noticed throughout our conversation how personally significant it was for her to introduce single mothers to her business opportunity because she saw it as a way to make their lives easier. She intimately understood the financial burdens of single parenthood, and helping women in similar situations gave her work yet another layer of personal significance. She referred to network marketing as a "people's franchise" since it required so little capital up front and allowed people who had never known success in their lives to really shine.

The Ecclesiastes Test

Because this lady was such an energetic person by nature, it was obvious that a job relying on a predictable daily routine wasn't for her. When I asked her what else about this company appealed to her, she said it gave her the opportunity to learn something new every day. You wouldn't be very successful if you didn't. Her next comment was key, because so many people can never imagine saying this on a Monday morning: "There's got to be a reason you wake up in the morning not saying 'I want to do this,' or 'I have to do this,' but 'I *get* to do this.'"

This is what I call the Ecclesiastes test. Very simply, do you enjoy what you are doing? As the writer of the book of Ecclesiastes expressed it, "There is nothing better for people than to be happy in their work" (Ecclesiastes 3:22 NLT).

Of the network-marketing "heavy hitters," I've noticed they all share certain traits. They all have strong family attachments and want a lifestyle that allows them to spend more time at home. They all share a fierce need for independence and thrive on the feeling they get from selling something they believe in. They also tend to see themselves as nonconformists and are attracted to a business model that makes one the CEO of her own company in one day.

A few of these people I spoke with described the sense of loneliness and isolation they'd experienced earlier in the corporate world, where they felt it was all about getting ahead at the expense of others. In many cases, they felt they were doing people a disservice by *not* making them aware of their business opportunity. Others mentioned that they'd never encountered a business opportunity that depended so much on cultivating other people's talents. They found work that they finally enjoy doing, which also allows them to enjoy life more.

I was often surprised by the inspirational tones many used to describe their work, using words like *transformational* and even *visionary*. Ah, there's that word again. One of network marketing's most successful distributors explained it this way: you have all the makings of explosive growth, but you have to drive it the way a visionary entrepreneur does. Such people look at every opportunity that presents itself throughout the course of their lives, and they evaluate each one in a visionary way. As is the case with so many highly successful business leaders, they see no discrepancy between their own personal beliefs and those of the organizations they represent. In other words, they get to do this work. They don't have to do it.

The Ecclesiastes Test:

Do you enjoy what you are doing?

I understand this feeling of enjoying what I do now. I absolutely love to write and tell stories (sorry I never made it as an engineer or geophysicist, Dad!), and I especially enjoy getting to pick up my kids from school every day.

Before You Quit the Day Job

Sometimes it's difficult to find a new job when you're already working, especially if you're putting in crazy hours at work, you're completely burned out when you get home, and the weekends are filled with family activities—or worse yet, you're missing those family activities because you have to work. Before quitting your job, regardless of how desperate you are to do so, it's critical to evaluate a few things in your personal life first. (Take it from me, these are extremely important things to consider.)

Family: If you're married, talk to your spouse about your decision. Try to get his feedback. Your husband will hopefully support your decision to quit your current job so you can find your dream job. I have a friend whose husband continuously quits his six-figure jobs without coming to her first and discussing the consequences. As a result, her life has been uprooted on several occasions as he moves from city to city, trying to find his dream job. It's not fair to the other person in your life when you selfishly do only what you want to do without considering how it will affect your loved ones.

Finances: This is where many people get tripped up. When a friend planned to quit her job, she landed a freelance writing gig the day she made her decision. At the time, she thought, *Wow, this really worked out. It must be fate.* So she handed in her resignation, believing that since this job came so easily, more would follow. Unfortunately, that one assignment was the only job she had for nearly three months. She wasn't prepared financially and went two months with no income and no savings to speak of. It was devastating and debt-inducing. Since freelancing is unpredictable and sporadic, she quickly discovered that it was wise to have at least six months to a year of cash stashed away to pay your estimated bills. Only you can determine what you can and cannot live on until you find that right job.

If you're a single mother, you'll definitely need to come up with a major plan of action that will provide you the finances to follow your dream. This can be done, but it will take planning on your part.

Consequences versus Benefits: Depending upon what career you go into, you may or may not take a drastic hit to your pocketbook. Money isn't everything, and it surely doesn't buy you happiness, but you need to decide if giving up money for more control over your life will ultimately be better.

Although my freelance friend misses the good money, she also has something she never had in her previous job: flexibility, family time, and the opportunity to work from home in her pjs. Consider consequences *and* benefits, then determine if the time or the decision is right.

Timeline: Determine when will be a good time to make your career change. This goes back to the issues of children, family, and money. You may desperately want to hand in your two-weeks notice tomorrow, but now that you know how much you have to put away in your savings, it may not be feasible. After determining how much you'll need to save, you can now set a date for Quitting Day. It's coming . . . it just might be further away than you like!

Plan of Action: What they say about setting goals is true. I have set many goals that were never truly achieved, but I think I confused goals with wishful thinking. Make sure you distinguish your goals from that type of thinking. It's still okay to write down your dreams, desires, wishes, and hopeful outcomes, but it's even more important to come up with a plan of action to make those very things a reality. Ask yourself these simple questions and write down your answers:

- What is it that I really want or would love to do? If you're not sure, don't worry; that answer may come only with prayer and time.

- What do I need to do in order to do what I love? Do I need to go back to school? Is it something I can teach myself? Do I already have a natural talent in this area? Is it possible I can reduce my hours to part-time so I can go back to school or look for a new job?

- Is there someone I know who I can talk to about getting a job in this field? Is there someone with whom I can network? Are there forums, bulletins, or websites I can join to start networking to learn how to break into the business?

▶ How much money have I already saved? (If none, don't fret; there's still hope.) If I need to save money so I can quit, how much do I have to save, and how long will that take?

▶ What am I willing to sacrifice? What are the things I'm not willing to sacrifice?

Once you've come up with your lists or answered the questions, try searching local papers or the internet for jobs that may involve some of the things you like to do.

Then start to think about the type of environment you want to work in:

▶ Do you want to work for a large company?

▶ Do you want to work in a large office or a small one or on your own at home?

▶ Do you want to feel like part of a team, or are you a loner?

▶ Do you want to work for a Fortune 500 company?

▶ Do you want or need flexibility?

▶ Do you want the option to work from home, even if it's for a company?

▶ Do you want to create your own company?

▶ What corporate values and ethics are important to you in your new job?

▶ How much time do you want to invest in your job, as opposed to other priorities, such as family?

▶ What type of people would you love to work with?

After you've answered these questions, if you still feel confused, there are many other tools, tests, and educational resources to help you find the right job that's perfect for you. WorldWideLearn .com explains how career-assessment tests work: "Your talents, abilities, values, likes and dislikes are all measured to narrow down the choices to jobs that fit your lifestyle interests. As a result, the feedback will give you an opportunity to explore careers that you'll enjoy and find highly motivating and personally rewarding."[5]

Taking the Leap

Changing careers doesn't have to be scary. This is an exciting time in your life, regardless of your age, family, or financial situation. Even if you've come to the conclusion that you may need to put your dream on hold for a few months, at least you'll be taking the necessary steps in getting one step closer.

So what are your options now that you've decided what it is that you really want to do? There are many things to consider.

Your current job: If you like where you're currently working but don't necessarily like the job you're doing, consider the possibility of moving positions within the same company. This way you can keep your benefits intact, and you'll be ahead of any newcomer because you already know the business or product. If staying with your current employer is an option, discuss your ideas with your boss or supervisor. See what the options are for moving into another department or even another office in a different city (if moving is an option for you). Don't be afraid to venture out of your own backyard.

If you lack the skills necessary for your new job, ask your employer about tuition reimbursement. Many companies will pay for your schooling but only if you attend a school for careers that can be utilized within the company. You typically have to achieve and maintain a C average in order for the company to pay for your classes. The NBC affiliate I worked for helped pay for my graduate degree.

The internet also provides us with many incredible opportunities to get a degree online without having to leave the comforts of our own homes. It also allows you to create your own schedule. No longer do you have to disrupt your life by trying to find time to go to class. The online class forum is an excellent option for a woman with a family.

However, online classes aren't for everyone, and not every degree can be achieved through these types of classes. If this is the case for your situation, you may need to find the time to actually show up at classes. If you haven't attended college before, be prepared for long hours of homework and studying. Since most of your courses are condensed into only one or two classes a week, you'll be required to put in a lot of reading, writing, and projects. If you have a family, you'll need to work out a schedule with your spouse that will allow you the time necessary to finish those assignments. Only you can work out a schedule that works best for your unique situation.

Gaining experience: There are also more inexpensive ways to learn the business you're interested in. Let's say you work in packaging as a data-entry clerk and you want to be in advertising. You've concluded there's no way you can afford to go to college, nor do you have the time to invest. What should you do?

Don't give up hope. You already have talent and experience; it just may not be in the field you want to be in. And you have basic skills that can get your foot in the door to any other type of business.

In his article "Finding the Right Career: Defining the Job That Is Best for You" on HelpGuide.org,[6] Pat McHenry Sullivan suggests some unique ways to gain experience in your desired field:

Identify resources in the community: Check out community colleges, your local chamber of commerce, and your state's job-development programs for opportunities for low-cost or free training. The Small Business Administration and other government agencies often offer free or inexpensive training in many skills.

Volunteer or work part-time: Do volunteer or part-time work that allows you to develop new skills and get recommendations and referrals while on the job.

Start looking for jobs you're qualified for at companies that are geared toward your ideal job. Using the advertising example, look for data-entry or clerical jobs at advertising or marketing firms. A lot of administrative jobs in these types of industries want someone to come in who has a desire to learn the business.

Be realistic: When you don't have the experience or schooling, you will need to invest time in getting one or the other before something major happens. That's just being realistic. If you expect things to happen overnight, you'll be sadly disappointed and will eventually feel defeated and ultimately give up all hope.

It's great to dream big, but take that big dream and break it down into baby steps.

Looking at your search for your talents in this way will help you understand that books and career counseling can take you only so far. Personality-assessment tests are great for helping to identify our "skill sets" and basic occupational preferences, but they don't tap into your deeper emotional framework. Listen for the "whisper." Be aware of that soft voice leading you in the right direction. Once we begin to think of our true talents as a process by which we dedicate ourselves to connecting with our deepest passions and our true God-given purpose, the more valuable these career tools will become.

When I first graduated from college, I had degrees in both business and journalism. My heart was in journalism, but the number of rejection letters I was collecting from news stations was growing every day. I didn't think I would ever get a paying job, and the lure of security in financial services was appealing. That's when I was offered a position with a financial company and was flown to Atlanta for the final interviewing process. During that time, human-resource managers showed the candidates a video of how wonderful the company was. Truly, I was more interested in the video and the storytelling than any job there. That's when I heard the whisper. *Keep going. You may be rejected again and again, but it takes only one yes.*

So I kept sending out my resume, and finally, just days away from Christmas of 1986, I got a call from a little news station in San Angelo, Texas. KLST-TV needed a weekend anchor/reporter/producer/videographer/editor/writer, etc. In other words, someone who didn't mind working long, long hours. A wonderful man named Don

Scott gave me my first break in TV, and I loved every hard-working minute of it. I made half the salary I would have made in the business job, but I didn't care. I drove my dad's old Plymouth Valiant, which my friends said looked like something out of a funky B-52's rock-music video. At least I didn't have my hair in a beehive, but my parents did send me a new outfit now and then, so I didn't have to wear the same suit every weekend. It sure wasn't perfect, but I was thrilled!

Listen for the whisper. The process takes both commitment and patience, and it's best to start preparing now. Don't wait for a giant epiphany. Try to be both optimistic and realistic, remembering that the process is largely trial-and-error. Try to be patient with yourself even if you don't have all the answers a year from now. Keep going. Remember that most people find their true calling only after overcoming difficulty, and many made mistakes before eventually getting it right. But anything this important is worth pursuing because the reward—time invested in purposeful, fulfilling, enjoyable work—depends on it.

ACTION APPLICATION

After meeting with your CEO, God, and thinking through some of the questions in this chapter, write a job description that details your ideal job. Something that reflects your values and passions. This is your chance to dream. Below are some practical tools to help get you started on making this a reality.

More Resources

If it's been a while since you've recently looked for a job, you may be unfamiliar with the job market. Job searching is time-consuming, and there are so many job resources to search through. But I have a couple of links to websites that will help you save time. All you have to do is type in the job title you're seeking and the city you're looking in, and the site does all the work for you by providing an extensive list of jobs with that title or similar titles from thousands of job databases including monster.com, craigslist.org, hotjobs, and CareerBuilder. It will also provide actual company website listings, so this makes your job search so much easier. Try these links:

- www.about.com/careers/

- www.indeed.com

Now consider when you'll find the time to actually interview. A lot of companies nowadays are screening applicants through an initial phone interview.

Also, depending on your dream job, you may have to travel to another city for your interview. Here are a couple of cool sites to check out:

- www.LiveCareer.com

- http://jobsearch.about.com/od/careertests/a/careertests. htm

ACTION APPLICATION

And here's a site that provides numerous options for career testing:

- http://tools.monster.com

After you've taken a career-assessment test and received your list of potential jobs that fit your criteria, research jobs that sound interesting by visiting the Occupational Outlook Handbook at www.bls .gov/oco/. You can look for just about any job title on this website, and it will provide the following information about that particular job:

- The nature of the job, which includes the tiniest details and responsibilities involved

- The job environment

- The training, schooling, and other qualifications you would need in order to get a job in this field (plus the kind of advancement opportunities you may have)

- The job market for the particular job

- A job outlook that gives you an idea of what the future holds for the job

- Median annual earnings

- Related occupations

- Places to go for additional information

9

Time for
Money Matters

*The most common way people give up their power
is by thinking they don't have any.*

—ALICE WALKER, AUTHOR OF *THE COLOR PURPLE*

I t's the stuff couples fight about. It steals our years in terms of worry, frustration, and lost opportunity. It's one of our greatest investments of time—yet managing money often ranks lowest on our priority list.

We found in our survey that women spent an average of twenty-six hours per week at work (a figure that includes women who don't work outside of the home)—but only one hour a week taking responsibility for the fruit of that labor. (The notable exception in our survey was younger women—eighteen to twenty-four years old—who work part-time. Women in this category reported investing an average of five hours weekly in managing money. However, the survey included only a small sample size of women working part-time in that age range.)

**Time Spent on Investments by Women
in Survey Based on Age and Work Status**

| Does not work | Part-time | Full-time * |

*Work status according to age

** Average number of hours spent on investments per week

We also found that women working full-time with children spent nearly three times as many hours per week on investing than full-time workers without children. (Find out more about this study at carolyncastleberry.com.) This might reflect these women's planning for their own retirement as well as for their children's education.

While women ranked money management low on their priority list, we clearly know that poor money management is one of our greatest time stealers. Here's what some of the Overwhelmed women wrote:

"I don't make enough money, so I have to spend way too much time on my work, trying to make more money, so it takes away time from everything else."

"I have to spend too much time at a job I absolutely hate making poverty-level wages and no insurance of any kind to barely get by."

"I have entirely too much stress because I don't seem to have enough time and money to be putting it in the right places."

And here's a comment from a Pressured lady: "To the extent that it lies in my own hands, I think I manage my time very well. However, my employer pretty much 'owns' me. I have a management-level job, which we need in order to stay afloat financially, so I put in many hours."

One Procrastinator wrote that "free flowing finances" was preventing her from better managing her time.

These comments and survey results may help explain a frightening statistic from the National Center for Women and Retirement Research (NCWRR): of women thirty-five to fifty-five years old, between one third and two thirds will be impoverished by age seventy. Also, women live an average of seven years longer than men. That means many of us will have no choice but to personally handle our own finances at some point.

And though I'm addressing the investment of money here, really the larger question is how we invest the much more valuable currency of time. You've heard the expression that time is money; let me turn that around and say that money is time. Becoming a good steward of your resources will literally help you buy time so you don't have to invest your years in a job you hate.

The controversial area of God and money makes news. Not long ago the cover line on *Time* magazine read, "Does God Want You to Be Rich?" The writers put together a list of seemingly contradictory verses of Scripture highlighting God's material blessings, like this one, "Be careful not to say in your heart, 'My power and strong hand have made me rich.' But remember the Lord your God. For it is He Who is giving you power to become rich. By this He may keep His agreement which He promised to your fathers, as it is this day" (Deuteronomy 8:17–18 NLV).

The "other side" was presented in verses like this one: "Do not store up for yourselves treasures on earth, where moth and rust destroy, and where thieves break in and steal. But store up for yourselves treasures in heaven, where neither moth nor rust destroys and where thieves do not break in or steal; for where your treasure is, there your heart will be also" (Matthew 6:19–21 NASB).

As I read through these biblical passages, I didn't see any contradiction. In fact, money is one of the hot topics of the Bible, with more than two thousand verses referencing finances or possessions, and I still don't see any contradiction. What I do see is money placed in the right perspective and priority—under God. Let me break it down into three spiritual principles of money.

It's Our Responsibility

In reading the *Time* article, I felt that the writers missed the important points about God and money. In inquiring whether the Lord wants us all to be rich, they were asking the wrong question! Our real financial questions are these: Will I be able to pay my bills? Can I get out of debt? Will I have enough money to support myself during retirement? Will I ever be able to retire? Am I responsible and a good steward of what I've been given?

Women are facing a financial crisis in this country, and God cares deeply about this. He never intended us to live in debt or without enough resources to provide for us during our retirement. On the contrary, would you believe that the world's first female investor is seen in the Bible in Proverbs 31? Her example shows modern women how to create, consider, and invest our way to financial security. This woman created products, considered her field of investment (real estate), then actually bought the field with her earned income (her day job). She went on to improve her investment and turn it into a vineyard to create something called passive income—money working for her instead of the other way around. It was also an investment that had multiple uses in her society and would help take care of her family for generations to come. Not a bad investment of money and time.

God wants interest on his investment, especially the time he's given each of us on earth.

Her investment approach is also consistent with the teachings of Jesus on money. Remember the parable of the talents we looked at earlier? God is watching what we do with what we've been entrusted with, and he hopes we'll multiply our resources—whatever they are. He wants interest on his investment, especially the time he's given each of us on earth.

Someday, when we face the Big Boss, we don't want to end up saying, "Look, I played it safe. I didn't take any chances. I buried my true talents in the ground." Instead he wants to hear, "Lord, I stepped out in faith! I took my talents (whatever they are) and turned them into time well spent for you. I multiplied all the resources you gave me so you would have a huge return on your investment." It's our job to be good stewards of money. And money is time.

Money Is Not the Goal

Does God promise riches to everyone who follows him? Yes! But not necessarily financial riches.

The apostle Paul writes, "We are poor, but we give spiritual riches to others. We own nothing, and yet we have everything" (2 Corinthians 6:10, *THE BOOK*). God calls us to a life of sacrifice along with blessing. Jesus also says that he came that we might have life and have it *abundantly* (see John 10:10). Yes, that can mean abundant life in every way, including financially. But remember even Jesus had "no place to lay his head" (Matthew 8:20 NIV). I would also argue that one of the richest women to ever live was Mother Teresa. Money is an area of life, just like any other, that the Lord will help us with if we ask him, and he never intended us to be slaves to finances or jobs we hate. He intends for us to use money for good purposes.

We also have to face the harsh reality that money itself will never bring true happiness or stability. You've probably heard the misquoted verse from the Bible, "Money is the root of all evil." Wrong. The problem isn't money, but *loving* money: "The love of money is a root of all sorts of evil" (1 Timothy 6:10 NASB). Pursuing money just for money's sake is like a never-ending thirst that can't be quenched. The Bible goes on to say, "He who loves money will not be satisfied with money, nor he who loves abundance with its income" (Ecclesiastes 5:10 NASB). The Bible consistently teaches us that nothing is to come before God on our priority list, including money.

If we're brutally honest with ourselves, keeping finances in perspective is a real problem. As I mentioned, money is consistently a leading cause of conflict for American couples. Don't we spend a majority of our time in money-making activities, like careers or more education to bring more money into the house?

And yet the Bible makes it clear that money is not the first goal:

Do not store up for yourselves treasures on earth, where moth and rust destroy, and where thieves break in and steal. But store up for yourselves treasures in heaven, where neither moth nor rust destroys, and where thieves do not break in or steal. . . . No one can serve two masters; for either he will hate the one and love the other, or he will be devoted to one and despise the other. You cannot serve God and wealth. (Matthew 6:19–20, 24 NASB)

Money can never be first on our priority lists. That's *God's* position: "Seek first His kingdom and His righteousness" (Matthew 6:33 NASB). God is always first.

As I put the business degree aside and really learned how money works, the Lord kept leading me back to the lady in Proverbs 31 who knew how to put money in its place: it was a priority, but not first priority. She prospered financially by building a business and investing in real estate but didn't let it affect her heart or desire for God. This right perspective allowed her to "sense that her gain was good" and to "smile at the future" without forgetting that her true spiritual riches and stability were in God. The Lord is very jealous of our time and our attention. Focusing your mind on material riches is a big mistake. The focus should be on what money can do . . . not money itself.

The Test of Giving

This leads us to a spiritual principle of money that tests our faith and always brings a return on our investment. When we give to God first, he always gives back. And in the measure we give, we also receive. In fact, giving is the only area in the Bible where God actually tells us to test him:

> "Bring the tenth part into the store-house, so that there may be food in My house. Test Me in this," says the Lord of All. "See if I will not then open the windows of heaven and pour out good things for you until there is no more need." (Malachi 3:10 NLV)

When you give to anyone, it's as if you're giving to Jesus himself. That's the heart of giving financially to God. You may be able to fool everyone, but not him. When the Israelites wanted to know how they were dishonoring God, he told them (through Malachi) that they were cheating him in their finances—"by taking your prize animals to market for top dollar, but bringing blind, lame and half-dead ones to my altar" (Malachi 1:7–8 TLB). Robbing God with your money deeply offends him, and it also robs you of the blessings he wants to bring into your life.

If you want to start getting out of debt, give first to God. If you want to build a business, give first to God. If you want enough income to carry you through your retirement years, give first to God. Don't pay yourself first, as most financial advisers will tell you. Pay God first, and just watch what he does in your life. You simply cannot outgive him.

It wasn't until I started taking this much more seriously that I finally experienced the joy and true wealth that God offers to everyone who will step up to the plate when it comes to giving. I finally made the decision to give 10 percent out of my gross income, not my net income. This meant God got paid before Uncle Sam—and, most significant, before me. Scary! My faith was pretty shaky at the time, so I set up a separate account for God (to keep me on the straight-and-narrow financial path) and used it for all my charitable giving.

You may have heard the following story before, but I'll tell it again: just like everyone I know who has made this decision—yes, *everyone*—God blessed me remarkably. I actually had money left over after giving to God's work and paying my bills. I kept checking the account again and again to make sure I hadn't missed anything. I was giving more than I ever had, but I had more money left over.

Financial giving is a consistent theme in both the New and Old Testaments, including the Proverbs 31 investor who was then able to spend her time giving back. She "extends her hand to the poor; and she stretches out her hands to the needy" (Proverbs 31:20 NASB). Not only was she providing for her family, she was investing time contributing to her community. And that brings more than just financial joy.

I've watched churches make a huge impact on communities through the right use of money. On television I profiled a group called Orphan Helpers, and it's made a huge impact on me. It's reaching out to the poorest of the poor around the world and doing so through the financial expertise and business skills of those educated in the right use of money. CBN's Operation Blessing has delivered more than 10 million pounds of food and household products to people in need and provided health care and $22 million in free medicine to destitute people. These are financial resources from thousands of people making a tremendous difference. That's when money can be a blessing—when it's in correct relationship to God, submitted to his will.

Now let me take the test of giving to an entirely new level. What would you do if the Lord asked you to give up everything for him?

Earlier we touched on a tough and controversial passage in Mark 10, but let's look again:

> As Jesus started on his way, a man ran up to him and fell on his knees before him. "Good teacher," he asked, "what must I do to inherit eternal life?"
>
> "Why do you call me good?" Jesus answered. "No one is good—except God alone. You know the commandments: 'Do not murder, do not commit adultery, do not steal, do not give false testimony, do not defraud, honor your father and mother.'"
>
> "Teacher," he declared, "all these I have kept since I was a boy."
>
> Jesus looked at him and loved him. "One thing you lack," he said. "Go, sell everything you have and give to the poor, and you will have treasure in heaven. Then come, follow me."
>
> At this the man's face fell. He went away sad, because he had great wealth.
>
> Jesus looked around and said to his disciples, "How hard it is for the rich to enter the kingdom of God!"
>
> The disciples were amazed at his words. But Jesus said again, "Children, how hard it is to enter the kingdom of God! It is easier for a camel to go through the eye of a needle than for a rich man to enter the kingdom of God." (Mark 10:17–25 NIV)

Wow! Tough words! And this is where the story usually stops, including how it was referred to in the *Time* magazine article. But read on, dear friends. Jesus' disciples asked the question you're probably pondering right now:

The disciples were even more amazed, and said to each other, "Who then can be saved?"

Jesus looked at them and said, "With man this is impossible, but not with God; all things are possible with God."

Peter said to him, "We have left everything to follow you!"

"I tell you the truth," Jesus replied, "no one who has left home or brothers or sisters or mother or father or children or fields for me and the gospel will fail to receive a hundred times as much in this present age (homes, brothers, sisters, mothers, children and fields—and with them, persecutions) and in the age to come, eternal life. But many who are first will be last, and the last first." (Mark 10:26–31 NIV)

Did you hear that? That's a 100 percent rate of return on his investment. In God's way. But the rich guy was so focused on his own security that his mind was closed to the possibilities right in front of him.

Also note that word *persecutions* that Jesus used. With God's big dreams, you'll also experience trials, if you're a true follower of Christ. And if you read the book of Revelation, you'll see that a time will come when Christians won't be able to buy and sell anything in the general market. In that time, money will mean absolutely nothing. Can you wrap your mind around that?

In the meantime, we're instructed to use money for good, to keep it in proper perspective, and always be willing to give. Remember these words from Jesus:

I tell you, use the riches of this world to help others. In that way, you will make friends for yourselves. Then when your riches are gone, you will be welcomed into your eternal home in heaven. (Luke 16:9 NIRV)

Test him in this. Give first to God and just see how he blesses your life—spiritually, emotionally, and yes, financially.

Have You Ever Thought about Tithing Time?

▹ **Volunteer at your church or synagogue.**

▹ **Volunteer at your child's school.**

▹ **Volunteer with an orphan ministry. Here are three that I love:**

    1. **ORPHANetwork (http://orphanetwork.net)**

    2. **Orphan Helpers (www.orphanhelpers.com)**

    3. **Orphans Promise (www.ob.org/orphanspromise)**

Three Steps to Turn Money into Time

To date I've written two books, numerous articles, and even more newsletters on the topic of money. In saying that money is time, I mean that a healthy relationship with your finances will give you the power to make choices in your life. When you stop being a slave to wages and learn to manage the resources God has given, you also realize how you're the manager of your time. Here are three principles to get started turning money into a much more valuable asset—your time well spent.

Give It Time

"The trustworthy person will get a rich reward, but a person who wants quick riches will get into trouble" (Proverbs 28:20 NLT). If anyone tells you she has a surefire way to solve all your financial problems and get rich quickly, I have one word for you: *RUN!* How do I know this? Well, because one year my husband and I heard a pitch just like this, and we didn't run. What we lost in dollars, we did gain in wisdom. Here it is: you'll save more time if you give yourself more time.

You know the story. You may have lived it yourself. A dear friend who was well known and respected in the community was approached by a man who promised big bucks for little effort. We listened to his pitch about a web-based business that was "guaranteed" to quickly make thousands of extra dollars in income every month.

As I was listening to the pitch, I knew he was a fraud. Every cell in my body was screaming for me to exit the room. But I wanted to be nice and didn't want to offend anyone or make our friend uncomfortable by walking out. So we stayed, invested the money—then never saw the guy again, or the big bucks he promised.

Here's the truth that many of us don't want to hear: building financial security takes time. Building anything worthwhile takes time. The problem is that in our fast-paced, buy-now-pay-later society, we don't want to take the time. Another gem of wisdom from King Solomon reminds us that "dishonest money dwindles away, but he who gathers money little by little makes it grow" (Proverbs 13:11 NIV). The key here is "little by little."

If You Don't Understand It, Don't Waste Your Time

One more reason we should have run from that get-rich-quick deal is that neither my husband nor I really understood it. The salesman spoke a mile a minute and made very little sense. At the time, I worked as a TV reporter, and I couldn't resist asking one question, especially when this man compared himself to Bill Gates. Hello! But he took my question as a personal affront and insinuated that all this investment stuff was really over my head anyway. I kept quiet for the remainder of the meeting. Another bad move.

One of my investment rules to live by was echoed by an investment counselor I interviewed for the *Living the Life* program. Doreen Roadman, of JJ Schopen & Associates in Virginia Beach, expressed it simply: "If you don't understand it, don't do it." Smart lady. But putting her words into practice takes humility. Just like anyone learning a new skill, you have to take baby steps before you can walk, before you can run in the investment world. You aren't going to know and understand everything in one day. And, yes, at times you're going to fail. I don't know one person who hasn't made some sort of mistake with money. But failure can be our most poignant teacher.

Take Time to Find Your Field

During an interview for a Canadian program called *100 Huntley Street,* reporter Moira Brown said to me, "So, Carolyn, basically you're telling me that I have to go look for a field." Well . . . yes, I am. As I mentioned, I base my financial principles on the model God has given us through the Proverbs 31 woman. She was a businessperson and a real-estate investor, and she gave herself time to search for and consider her field of investment, which was real estate, before ever investing a dime.

During a production meeting for *Living the Life,* prior to one of my financial segments on women and investing, one of the other women told me, "My problem is I don't have time to learn about investing . . . not with children and a job!" My response was this: "You don't have to know everything about investing; you just have to understand your 'field,' just like the smart investor from Proverbs 31."

Today women have so many more options when it comes to finding a field of investment. In *Women, Get Answers About Your Money* I write in-depth about four fields, including real estate, investing in your own business, the stock market, and intellectual property. Before ever investing in my first income-producing property, I spent two years studying the field of real estate.

Begin by paying attention to the financial world around you and especially to those investments that work for the long-term. From watching financial news channels to attending a seminar; from reading a book on money to joining an investment club that turns education into action—you don't have to spend a great deal of time on this. Perhaps you can start with just fifteen minutes, three days a week.

Who has time to learn about investing? You do! Because managing money is something you'll always have to deal with while you're on this earth. Always. You'll feel frightened and overwhelmed at first, but keep going. Keep learning. Keep praying because the God of all resources knows what you need, and he cares about every detail of your life, including your time invested in money.

ACTION APPLICATION

Ask yourself . . .

1. How much time each day do I spend making money?

2. How much time each week do I spend worrying or fighting about money?

3. How much time each week do I spend investing that money?

4. What one step can I take today to become a good steward of my resources?

5. How can I invest my time and money in something that matters to God and me?

10

Now Is Your Time

Christ has set us free to live a free life. So take your stand!
Never again let anyone put a harness of slavery on you.

—GALATIANS 5:1 MSG

As I mentioned when we began this journey, this is the verse of Scripture I held on to when I chose to walk away from being a wage slave in a job that was increasingly stealing my most precious asset—my time with my little family. That's when I remembered that my true freedom has already been bought for me, paid for by the death and resurrection of Jesus. The questions I asked myself began to change. Instead of, "What should I do with my time?" I began asking, "To whom should I look for answers?" That led me back to studying the Bible as I never had before—as a practical guide for daily life and success.

The apostle Paul sums it up nicely:

I'm not saying that I have this all together, that I have it made. But I am well on my way, reaching out for Christ, who has so wondrously reached out for me. Friends, don't get me wrong: By no means do I count myself an expert in all of this, but I've got my eye on the goal, where God is beckoning us onward—to Jesus. I'm off and running and I'm not turning back. (Philippians 3:12–14 MSG)

If God set up this entire plan, why not begin your journey toward freedom by looking to the one who thought you up in the first place—the one who formed and executed his plan for the earth simply by speaking a Word? God is encouraging all of us onward.

And do you know the most freeing part? God has it all figured out, so we don't have to worry. He has a vision that's uniquely suited to our talents and personalities. He has always had this vision for you. "We are God's workmanship, created in Christ Jesus to do good works, which God prepared in advance for us to do" (Ephesians 2:10 NIV). *Prepared in advance!* He has a plan for each of our lives, and he's happy to share it with us every day, if we'll just take the time to meet with him and develop this relationship.

I love how the apostle Paul admits that he doesn't have it all together, because, really, who does? The Bible says each of us has missed the mark of God's perfect will for our lives. The politically incorrect term for this is *sin*. In writing to the church in Rome, Paul spells it out: "All have sinned and fall short of the glory of God" (Romans 3:23 NIV). In other words, we've all been rebellious and stubborn in wanting our own way, and "the wages of sin is death" (Romans 6:23 NIV). But God bridged that gap by sending his Son to pay the high price for us:

Christ arrives right on time to make this happen. He didn't, and doesn't, wait for us to get ready. He presented himself for this sacrificial death when we were far too weak and rebellious to do anything to get ourselves ready. And even if we hadn't been so weak, we wouldn't have known what to do anyway. We can understand someone dying for a person worth dying for, and we can understand how someone good and noble could inspire us to selfless sacrifice. But God put his love on the line for us by offering his Son in sacrificial death while we were of no use whatever to him. (Romans 5:6–8 MSG)

It's hard to wrap your mind around, isn't it? That someone would love us that much, unconditionally. That true freedom really begins in a person.

So how do you begin your journey toward the life you were meant to have, eternally with God and abundantly here on earth? By simply asking. Christ says, "Behold, I stand at the door and knock; if anyone hears My voice and opens the door, I will come in to him and will dine with him, and he with Me" (Revelation 3:20 NASB). God really doesn't care about your words as much as your heart.

When I made this decision, I prayed a prayer like the one written by Campus Crusade for Christ:

Lord Jesus, I need You. Thank you for dying on the cross for my sins. I open the door of my life and receive you as my Savior and Lord. Thank you for forgiving my sins and giving me eternal life. Take control of the throne of my life. Make me the kind of person you want me to be.

If you pray this prayer, God also promises never to leave you or forsake you. You have his promise of eternal life. You also have his promise of true freedom.

My friends, time is really all we have. Why waste one more moment trying to figure everything out by yourself? There is one who has mastered the art of investing time daily, moment by moment—eternally—and he's hoping to share his time with you.

Where Does the Time Go?

DAY ONE	DAY TWO	DAY THREE
Morning		
6 a.m.		
7		
8		
9		
10		
11		
Afternoon		
12 p.m.		
1		
2		
3		
4		
5		

6		
7		
8		
9		
10		
11		
Early Morning		
12 a.m.		
1		
2		
3		
4		
5		

▶ Where are your greatest time traps?

▶ Where are you spending time where it matters most?

Personal Strategy Notes

My Top 10 Time Strategies

1.

2.

3.

4.

5.

6.

7.

8.

9.

10.

ACKNOWLEDGMENTS

As always, my first thank you belongs to my beloved Lord and Savior, Jesus Christ. He has given us the gift of time, and every day I'm grateful for it. I also want to thank my husband who often gave me the time to write this book, entertaining little ones at basketball games or playing chess while I wrote another chapter. To our children—the time I spend with you gives me the greatest joy in my life. I never dreamed I would be so blessed. To my parents— thank you so much for all the time you have given me and our family. You were always there.

Much gratitude goes to my agent, Wes Yoder of Ambassador Agency, who truly loves the Lord and is committed to quality work in honor of Christ. Thank you so much to the fantastic team at Howard Books, including senior editor Cindy Lambert and to editor Lisa Bergren, who, like a coach striving for excellence, encouraged me to become a more open and vulnerable writer. Special thanks to Thomas Womack, who first realized that in writing books about money, I was really writing about a much greater currency: time. My gratitude also goes to editor Jacki Payne, my first sounding board on all manuscripts, and to Corey Blake and Ed Erickson, who helped with research.

ACKNOWLEDGMENTS

A special thanks to the Christian Broadcasting Network and the wonderfully fun, creative staff of *Living the Life*. I love serving with you! And to all of you who now email me with encouraging words or story ideas, I can't tell you how much your time means to me. May God bless all of you abundantly and eternally in Jesus.

NOTES

Chapter One: Time Crunched

1. Gordon MacDonald, *Ordering Your Private World* (Nashville: Nelson, 2003), 81.

Chapter Two: This Is Your Time

1. Jackson Snyder, "The Dash between the Dates," www.jacksonsnyder.com/arc/Sermons%202/The%20Dash.htm.

Chapter Three: The Overwhelmed

1. Dan Thurmon, *Success in Action: The Direct Path to Your Higher Potential* (Atlanta: Action Press, 2005), 111, 115.
2. American Psychological Association. "Is Multitasking More Efficient?" press release, August 5, 2001, www.apa.org/journals/releases/xhp274763.pdf.
3. "Declutter 15 Minutes a Day—5 Great Tools That Make It Easy!"; www.flylady.net/pages/flyinglessons_decluttertips.asp. Accessed on April 7, 2008.
4. "Efficiency," radio transcript, *Redeeming the Time,* www.lifechangingseminars.com/radio_transcripts_eff.htm.

Chapter Four: The Procrastinators

1. Dr. Linda Mintle, phone interview, March 28, 2008.
2. Michael Kanellos, "MIT explains why bad habits are hard to break," CNET News, October 19, 2005, http://news.cnet.com/MIT-explains-why-bad-habits-are-hard-to-break/2100-11395_3-5902850.html.

3. Mary Ann Chapman, "BAD Choices," *Psychology Today,* September/October 1999, http://psychologytoday.com/articles/pto-19990901-000034.html.
4. Tracy Quinn, ed., *Quotable Women of the Twentieth Century* (New York: Adler Books, 1999), 219.
5. "The Wisdom of Norman Vincent Peale," www.USDreams.com/Peale W29.html.
6. Brian Tracy, "Transforming Bad Habits," SuccessMethods.org., http://successmethods.org/briantracy_a17.html.
7. David A. Gershaw, PhD, "Breaking Bad Habits," Jiskha Homework Help, www.jiskha.com.
8. Rita Emmett, *The Procrastinating Child: A Handbook for Adults to Help Children Stop Putting Things Off* (New York: Walker, 2002), 111, 124.
9. Kanellos, ibid.

Chapter Five: The Pressured

1. From Kathy Mitchell and Marcy Sugar, "Annie's Mailbox," *Virginian Pilot,* November 13, 2006.
2. "Decision Making," Wikipedia.org, http://en.wikipedia.org/wiki/Decision_making.
3. http://en.wikipedia.org/wiki/Decision_making#Cognitive_and_personal_biases_in_decision_making.
4. Bill Robinson, Whitworth College Spring 2004 Convocation Address, www.whitworth.edu/Administration/PresidentsOffice/Messages/Spring2004Convocation.htm.
5. Quinn, ed., *Quotable Women,* 219.
6. Dr. Charles Foster, *What Do I Do Now?: Dr. Foster's 30 Laws of Great Decision Making,* (New York: Simon & Schuster, 2001), http://llamagraphics.com/Meadow/Books/bookWhatdoIdoNow.html.
7. Mary Ellen Guffey, *Business Communication: Process and Product,* 2nd ed. (Cincinnati: South-Western College Publishing, 1996), chapter 1. http://guffey.swlearning.com/newsletter/archives/older/critical.html.
8. Business.gov, www.sba.gov/smallbusinessplanner/manage/makedecisions/serv_gooddec.html.
9. Henry Cloud, *9 Things You Simply Must Do to Succeed in Love and Life* (Brentwood, TN: Integrity, 2004), 71.
10. Edward de Bono, *6 Thinking Hats* (Boston: Little, Brown, 1985), http://www.mindtools.com/pages/article/newTED_07.htm.
11. Quinn, ed., *Quotable Women,* 82.

Chapter Six: The Self-Stressed

1. Henry Cloud, *The Secret Things of God: Unlocking the Treasures Reserved for You* (West Monroe, LA: Howard Books, 2007), 54.
2. http://www.christiangoth.com/whoyouare.html.
3. Christine Corelli, "Positive Attitude—Enough Already?" Written Word, www.christinespeaks.com. See www.christinespeaks.com/positive-atttitude-article.htm.
4. "Positive attitude delays aging," BBC News, September 9, 2004, http://news .bbc.co.uk/2/hi/health/3642356.stm.
5. "Positive Thinking: Practice This Stress Management Skill," Mayo Clinic, www.mayoclinic.com/health/positive-thinking/SR00009.
6. Karman Morey, "The Ability to Maintain a Positive Attitude," www .experientialdynamics.org/models/Kmorey.htm.
7. John Vestman, "Result Language," www.johnvestman.com/Result_language .htm.
8. Della Menechella, "I'm Not Depressed; I've Just Been Having a Lousy Conversation with Myself (Or How to Stop Your Words from Messing Up Your Life)," Personal Peak Performance Unlimited, www.dellamenechella .com/I'm%20Not%20Depressed.htm.
9. "Should Donald Trump Be Fired?" CBS News, www.cbsnews.com, and www.brainyquote.com/quotes/authors/d/donald_trump.html.

Chapter Seven: Time for Your Loved Ones

1. "Relationship Quotes," www.great-quotes.com/cgi-bin/viewquotes.cgi?keyword-anthony+robbins+relationships action-search.
2. Shankar Vedantam, "Social Isolation Growing in U.S. Study Says," *Washington Post*, June 23, 2006, www.washingtonpost.com/wp-dyn/content/article/2006/ 06/22/AR2006062201763.html.
3. Vedantam, "Social Isolation."
4. "The Aging Body," *Merck Manual, Home Edition,* www.merck.com/mmhe/ sec01/ch003/ch003d.html.
5. "Relationship Quotes," Think Exist.com, http://en.thinkexist.com, 1999–2006, http://en.thinkexist.com/quotes/Barbara_Bush/.
6. Dr. Brenda Shoshanna, "Seven Unfailing Laws of Happy Relationships," www.hodu.com/laws.html.

Chapter Eight: Time for Work That Matters

1. UCLA Higher Education Institute. "Spirituality in Higher Education," July 17, 2006, http://www.spirituality.ucla.edu/about/index.html.
2. C. D. Ryff, "Happiness is everything, or is it? Explorations on the meaning of psychological well-being," *Journal of Personality and Social Psychology* 57 (1989), 1069–81.
3. Corey Blake, telephone interview, July 11, 2006.
4. Po Bronson, *What Should I Do with My Life: The True Story of People Who Answered the Ultimate Question* (New York: Random House, 2002), 362.
5. "Career Assessment: What Are Your Skills, Motivations, Talents?"; www.worldwidelearn.com/career-assessment/index.html.
6. Pat McHenry Sullivan, M.A., *Finding the Right Career: Defining the Job That Is Best for You*, http://www.helpguide.org/life/finding_career.htm.

ABOUT THE AUTHOR

CAROLYN CASTLEBERRY is an international television co-host on the program *Living the Life,* airing on ABC Family and produced by the Christian Broadcasting Network. The program is also seen on Cornerstone TV Network, FamilyNet Television, and many local network affiliates. Carolyn reports on issues related to the family, including finances, health, and parenting. She's the author of *Women, Take Charge of Your Money: A Biblical Path to Financial Security* and *Women, Get Answers about Your Money: Because There Are No Dumb Questions about Personal Finance,* both published by Multnomah. She holds three degrees: two bachelor of science degrees in business and journalism from the University of Colorado and a master of arts degree from the College of William and Mary. She is also a real estate investor and has completed extensive education in real estate, including law, appraisal, finance, principles, and real estate practices.

Carolyn is an award-winning reporter and anchor who spent seventeen years working in news in Virginia and Colorado. Her reports have also aired on CNN, and her book has been featured on major media outlets, including *FOX & Friends,* PBS, the Canadian Broadcasting Corporation, and major print publications across the country. In Colorado she started the first national radio talk show for female executives on the Business Radio Network. For this effort, she was recognized by American Women in Radio and Television. Visit www.carolyncastleberry .com for more information.